Brent Barootes
WITH JANET GADESKI

REALITY CHECK

Straight Talk about
Sponsorship
Marketing

Library and Archives Canada Cataloguing in Publication

Barootes, Brent, 1961-, author
        Reality check : straight talk about sponsorship marketing / Brent Barootes and Janet Gadeski. -- First Canadian edition.

Includes bibliographical references and index.
ISBN 978-1-927375-18-1 (pbk.)

        1. Corporate sponsorship. 2. Fund raising--Management.
3. Nonprofit organizations--Marketing. 4. Nonprofit organizations--Finance. I. Gadeski, Janet, 1951-, author II. Title.

HD59.35.B37 2014   658.15'224   C2014-903113-0

Reality Check: Straight Talk about Sponsorship Marketing

Published by Civil Sector Press
Box 86, Station C, Toronto, Ontario, M6J 3M7 Canada

Telephone: 416-345-9403
www.charityinfo.ca

Publisher: Jim Hilborn
Edited by: Lisa MacDonald
Cover and book design: John VanDuzer, WISHART.NET

Brent Barootes

WITH JANET GADESKI

REALITY CHECK

Straight Talk about Sponsorship Marketing

Thank you to the love of my life and wife of over 13 years, Coryna and our beautiful and wonderful daughter, Brooklyn.

Both have endured my travel, long work hours and dedication to the industry for many years. They have supported me as I travelled for two or three weeks at a time to help clients and build my business. Without their understanding, I could not have accomplished a quarter of what I have been able to do.

B.B.

My work on **Reality Check** is dedicated to the social profit organizations whose work makes our world better – fairer, healthier, more educated, more beautiful.

I deeply appreciate Brent's expertise and generous sharing, not only in our collaboration but in his profession as well. Thank you, Brent, for choosing me as your writing collaborator.

J.G.

TABLE OF CONTENTS

Acknowledgements   ix

Preface   xiii

Introduction: The power of sponsorship   xiv

INVENTORY AND VALUATION   **1**

1   Beyond buildings: Identifying what properties can sell   5

2   What a property's assets are worth to potential sponsors   13

PROSPECTING   **21**

3   How to find your top candidate for a win-win sponsorship   25

DISCOVERY   **35**

4   Making discovery sessions work for you   39

5   Making the meeting or meetings work   41

PROPOSALS   **51**

6   Why custom proposals are best for properties and buyers   55

7   What to include: cover page; table of contents; about the sponsor;
     about you   59

8   What to include: Offer of benefits   67

9   What to include: Investment and discount; legal and closing   73

ACTIVATION – GETTING SPONSORS TO ACTIVATE   **83**

10   Why activation matters   87

11   Examples of activation tactics   93

12   Activation – Whose job is it and who pays?   99

FULFILLMENT MANAGEMENT   **105**

13   How to track fulfillment activities and report to your sponsor   107

SPONSOR SUMMITS   **121**

14   Making your sponsor summit a "can't miss" event   125

15   Reality: Better than you'd hoped   135

GLOSSARY   **137**

BONUS MATERIAL   **145**

Sample ONE – Inventory Valuation and Costing Template   146

Sample TWO – Inventory Asset Valuation Matrix   148

Sample THREE – Full Sponsorship Proposal   157

Sample FOUR – Fulfillment Spreadsheet   174

INDEX   **179**

BRENT'S ACKNOWLEDGEMENTS

When I undertook to write this book I knew it would require the collaboration of people whom I would ask to help me through the process, as well as being influenced by those who contributed (perhaps unknowingly) to my learning throughout the years.

But in truth, the influencers of this book extend way beyond my immediate circle of friends and esteemed colleagues and mentors. This group includes: all those small and large clients who, over a decade ago, trusted me and the Partnership Group – Sponsorship Specialists™ to serve them and help them succeed in the sponsorship world. Thank you to the folks that attended the Western Sponsorship Congress™ year after year enabling all of us to learn and share best practices.

I also think of the people who continue to believe in me and our company to guide them toward success in this industry. These are front-line people working daily with partners, suppliers and sponsors. These are the individuals who make an every-day difference in our industry and for whom I have written this book.

I would also like to dedicate this book to some institutions, without which none of this could have been possible. If IEG had not done the groundwork for the sponsorship industry over 25 years ago, there would be no industry. If the SMCC (Sponsorship Marketing Council of Canada) had not been formed to provide a single source voice and support for all members of our industry in Canada, we would not be as far along as we are. Events like the *Canadian Sponsorship Forum*, the *SMCC Marketing Awards,* the Sponsorship Toronto conference and other events, have all contributed to the development of this book.

And then there is Rotary. Over the years I have quoted the Rotary Four-Way Test as my personal motto and the guiding principles for the Partnership Group – Sponsorship Specialists™. Thank you to the Rotarians who have welcomed me as a member and taught me about service above self, and to those Rotary Clubs who have engaged us to help them to give back more to their communities.

And finally I would like to thank Janet Gadeski, my co-author for all her hard work and dedication to this project. She added her skilled interpretation to my knowledge to develop a book that people can read and learn from. I could not have done this on my own. Thank you, Janet.

JANET'S ACKNOWLEDGEMENTS

With a career spent in fundraising and charity leadership, I sit on the other side of the sponsorship fence. I introduced myself to Brent when I needed expert analysis of a controversy over some of the sponsorship policies of the 2010 Vancouver Olympics for Hilborn Charity eNEWS. I thought charities could learn something from that situation, but I soon discovered that Brent had much more to offer to charities and indeed any organization seeking sponsors.

Intrigued by his marketing-focused approach, and excited by his affirmation of what charities had to offer, I began writing more articles about his emphasis on the "business of sponsorship" and the tactics it required. I wanted charities to know that their supporters and audiences were an important market for sponsors. I wanted charities to negotiate sponsorships as confident equals. I wanted them to learn to listen for the unique needs of their sponsorship prospects and offer solutions that the prospects would gladly purchase with marketing dollars, not philanthropic pennies.

That led us eventually to this book – tangible proof that two passionate, opinionated individuals can listen to each other, learn from each other, and forge a respectful collaboration leading to a valuable outcome. In that, it is much like a successful sponsorship.

I am grateful for the unfailing support of my wonderful husband, **Gary Fisher**. His intellectual and artistic passions enrich my life, and his encouragement and belief in me has sustained me through many challenges.

I would also like to thank Jim Hilborn, founder of *Civil Sector Press* and *Hilborn Charity eNEWS*. He gave me the chance to write full-time about the sector I love, and he pays me for my opinions! Careers don't get much better than that.

PREFACE

In the past decade the sponsorship industry in Canada has grown exponentially. According to the *Canadian Sponsorship Landscape Study* (2013), just eight years ago sponsorship and experiential marketing accounted for a modest 5% of marketing budgets. Today, however, those categories claim over 20% of the dollars that Canadian corporations spend on marketing.

Traditionally, sports and events attracted most of the sponsorship dollars in Canada. Nonprofits sought sponsorship, but often as an act of philanthropy that did not address sponsors' business objectives. Then, across the board, brands (sponsorship buyers) began to say, "Give us value! Make sure there is a measurable, positive ROI. We are willing to support you, but you have to help us grow our business!" The landscape has changed, and it is no longer a game for amateurs.

Unfortunately the number of trained professionals with sponsorship buying or selling responsibilities is not keeping pace with the growth in sponsorship dollars. Training is available through the SMCC Western Sponsorship Congress™ and other professional development activities specific to the sponsorship industry. Also, organizations like the Association of Fundraising Professionals (AFP) include sponsorship as a break-out session in their conferences. However, this book is the result of a belief that more is needed – not everyone can afford to attend conferences or events like the SMCC One Day Sponsorship Training Workshops™.

Also, the sponsorship profession needs to reach a wider audience with the basic knowledge and understanding of how a property should run a successful sponsorship program. More webinars and workshops and conferences are not the solution. What this industry needs is a textbook on sponsorship for properties and rights holders. This is a how-to manual that shows those currently in the industry, those new to the industry, or those transitioning from philanthropy or other fields into the sponsorship industry how to "do it right." The vision was for a book written in plain language that included great examples and storytelling as well as tips, tools and proven success strategies - a book that would serve as a guide for individuals in the field and for post-secondary students studying sponsorship marketing.

And thus **Reality Check** was written. It is based on learning acquired from more than a quarter of a century of experience in the industry and almost two years of committed work and collaboration between various contributors and the co-authors. The end result is a book that can be used by students, industry leaders and newbies alike. We hope you enjoy it.

INTRODUCTION:
THE POWER OF SPONSORSHIP

Sponsorship is a very big business in Canada. The 2013 Canadian Sponsorship Landscape Study estimates that sponsors invested $1.57 billion in this form of marketing in 2012 with each sponsor that participated in the survey sponsoring, on average, 42 properties (recipients of sponsorships).

Every kind of business incorporates sponsorship in its marketing strategy. Huge corporations and small neighborhood businesses offer every product and service you can think of and they invest in everything – professional and amateur sports, fairs and festivals, charities and causes, municipal programs and facilities, the arts, education and environmental care.

With so much money and effort in the game, you might think that sponsorship is a successful, clear-cut endeavour. But it is not. Every year, many sponsors are disappointed in relationships, implementation and investment outcomes. And every year, properties overlook what they have to offer, what their audience, members or supporters are worth, and what their sponsors and potential sponsors really need.

The "secret" to a successful sponsorship isn't really a secret at all. It is something that would be evident if we took a moment to think about it – yet for some reason, most do not pause for that moment of thought when we approach our sponsorship strategy. Here it is in four simple sentences:

> Find out where your prospective sponsors hurt (i.e., what holds them back from greater success).
> Offer a customized solution at a fair market price.
> Go above and beyond to deliver.
> Repeat.

If that sounds a lot like the sales process – it is! Is sponsorship an important part of your revenue mix? Could it become important if you gave it more effort? You will achieve far better, longer-lasting results by selling solutions rather than begging for support. And the sponsorships you create when you take this approach will bring you not only more revenue, but more media coverage, more public awareness and more people – all to fuel your mission and achieve your own goals.

So –

> If you are ready to stop asking humbly for "support" and calling it "sponsorship"
> If you are willing to sell your sponsors specific benefits rather than giving them "the satisfaction of helping our good work"
> If you are willing to throw away your standardized gold, silver and bronze packages
> And above all, if you are ready to listen deeply and consistently to your sponsors,

then you are ready for the **Reality Check** that will set you on the path to a transformed sponsorship program.

Let's get started!

INVENTORY AND VALUATION

WHEN THE PEOPLE ON YOUR TEAM talk about sponsorship, what do the conversations sound like?

> "We have nothing to name – no buildings, no interesting equipment, no performances. Poor us! What could we ever offer a sponsor?"

Or –

> "Once we find a company that wants its name on our building, our sponsorship job is done."

Wrong both times! Every property, no matter how small, has assets. Even a showy, new building is just one asset among many that might be of interest to a sponsor. In this section, you will learn how to set aside your notions about what your property can or cannot offer, and instead identify dozens of opportunities with sales potential. Then you'll learn how to set an objective value on every asset, using formulas and valuations based on the experience of hundreds of corporate sponsors and sponsorship selling properties.

With that information in hand, you will be ready to sell – not ask for – the partnership your property deserves from the sponsors you can help most effectively. Doesn't that sound better than begging for a little help with the great work you do?

REALITY CHECK

REALITY CHECK – EVERY PROPERTY HAS SOMETHING TO SELL.

Consider this –

"Assets we've identified are our Christmas gift catalog, the annual 30-hour famine, and our youth ambassadors program. The last two Christmases, VISA has sponsored the goats in our online Christmas gift catalog." – **Neil Parekh**, *World Vision*

3

REALITY CHECK

Sponsoring goats? Yes! **Every** property has something to sell!

"We are on a busy intersection in downtown Calgary. Our marquee has value. One of our sponsors was an engineering firm with a low profile. They were growing rapidly, yet they couldn't get known. They wanted their name "on something" to strengthen their brand recognition. Now, they've been a series sponsor for six years with their name on our marquee, and it's really built their profile. It made people ask, "Who's that?" – **Suzanne Mott**, *Vertigo Theatre*

Vertigo Theatre could have limited its sponsorship vision to naming its building and its performance season. Instead, Suzanne worked with professional sponsorship counsel to identify additional high-value assets.

Are you convinced now? Good. Let's get down to work on your inventory.

1
BEYOND BUILDINGS:
IDENTIFYING WHAT PROPERTIES CAN SELL

When most people think of sponsorship, they think of naming rights because those are the most visible sign that a sponsor is involved. Naming an event or building creates an image of ownership or partnership for a sponsor. Examples of named properties include Toronto's Four Seasons Centre for the Performing Arts, Calgary's ScotiaBank Saddledome and Hamilton's Tim Hortons Field.

The next level is the ***presenting*** sponsorship. It is subordinate because it creates a lengthy name that is often shortened. Consider the difference between:

> The 2014 Toronto Shoppers Drug Mart Weekend to End Women's Cancers benefiting Princess Margaret Cancer Centre (naming rights), and
> Canadian Breast Cancer Foundation Run for the Cure, presented by CIBC (a presenting sponsorship).

It is all too easy for media, participants and even event staff and volunteers to drop the last few words on both events. When that happens, Shoppers Drug Mart stays, but CIBC vanishes. That makes a huge difference in the value of the sponsorship.

The presenting sponsorship is just one example of a subordinate sponsorship. With a named building, every inside space can also be named. For example, the Chan Centre for the Performing Arts at the University of British Columbia in Vancouver includes the Chan Shun Concert Hall, the Telus Studio Theatre and the Royal Bank Cinema.

Other subordinate sponsorships could be created for each performance stage at an outdoor music festival; a section, area or entry of a stadium; the curling rink, pool and gyms in a recreation centre; or a day, a weekend or a week of an event.

Both you and your prospects might ask whether there is really any value in subordinate sponsorships. Won't the visibility of the overall branding sponsor wash out the impact of the smaller ones?

The answer to this dilemma lies in building a package of assets that suits the business objectives of each individual prospect. Your prospect's budget matters, of course – it may not stretch to the amount required for a naming or title sponsorship. But during the discovery sessions, as you will see in Section 3, you can lead prospects to reveal their business objectives and challenges to you. Then you can choose from your list of all possible assets to create a customized subordinate sponsorship package that meets each prospect's needs and still honours your agreement with your principal sponsor.

POTENTIAL ASSETS FOR SPONSORSHIP

It bears repeating: **every** property has something to sell. Your property may be able to offer any or all of these and even more:

> Naming rights: title, presenting, major, or supporting sponsorships.

> The right to supply official products or be named as a preferred supplier. ("Official product" means that your property uses that product exclusively. "Preferred supplier" means you are not restricted to the sole use of that brand.)

> Category exclusivity bars your sponsor's competitors from eligibility as sponsors. When you give exclusivity, make sure the categories are defined and limited. For example, RBC is more than a bank. It has insurance and brokerage divisions as well. A contract with RBC should state whether the term "competitors" extends to other brokerages and insurance firms.

> The sponsor's use of the property's branding materials. Visible affiliation with a property that is respected or loved, such as a professional sports team or a high-impact children's charity, has great value for some sponsors.

> Merchandising rights (the right to create co-branded merchandise to sell) and product endorsements from the property.

> Discounts for multi-year contracts, rights of refusal for future sponsorship opportunities, performance incentives requiring the property to deliver certain measurable outcomes such as audience recall or coupon redemption.

INVENTORY AND VALUATION

> Planning input (but never control).

> Staging the property's event in the sponsor's venue. For example, when Canadian Tire sponsored the Livegreen Toronto festival, one of Canadian Tire's objectives was to encourage people to "feel good" about the retail company. The City of Toronto planned to disburse environmental initiative grants to community associations. As part of the Livegreen sponsorship, those grant presentations took place in Canadian Tire stores. Photos included the franchisee, the community representatives and the municipal councillor.

> Sampling, product demonstrations, sales, premium (gift) distribution and merchandising opportunities.

> Use of the property's logo, images and/or trademarks for the sponsor's promotion, advertising or other leveraged activities, or uniforms.

> Exclusive or non-exclusive identification in event signage (be sure to specify full, partial or non-broadcast view), on-site event signage, pre-event street flags and banners, press conference signage, vehicle signage.

> Tickets, passes and meet-and-greet opportunities for the sponsor's staff or clients.

> Event-related travel arrangements, administration, chaperone services such as airport greeters, ski hill ambassadors or theatre ushers, consumer prizes, and VIP or trade incentives.

> Experiences that money cannot buy; for example, the chance to meet a star performer or athlete backstage or after the game, a walk-on part in a theatre production, or meeting an award-winning researcher at a cancer foundation.

> Customized experiences. Perhaps your property has expertise that would benefit the sponsor, or vice-versa. For example, a post-secondary education institution created professional development opportunities such as a custom-built course in project management for sponsors'

employees. Its sponsors have provided guest lecturers for students and the area's business community, thereby introducing their company to potential recruits and customers.

> Property content for the sponsor's website, space for the sponsor on the property's website, interactive leads from contests on the property's website linking to the sponsor's website, and naming rights to an event website or microsite.

> Preferential, exclusive or early access for the sponsor and select customers.

> A block of tickets or parking spaces.

> Mailing and email list access within the bounds of privacy and anti-spam legislation, opportunities for sponsor inserts in the property's direct mail packages.

> Opportunities for draws and contests that generate new names for the sponsor's database.

> Benefits for the sponsor's employees, such as discounts, merchandise, partial "ownership" such as an employee-built and staffed water station at a marathon, access to the property's celebrity or other spokesperson, a special day for staff, a donation on behalf of the employees, or a volunteer program tailored for the sponsor's employees.

> Help for the sponsor's staff recruitment – perhaps a sponsor recruiting station at an event, distribution of recruitment information through the property's audience, or employee recruitment information in the property's mailing.

> Fringe benefits such as tickets, invitations, signage and sampling at other events or properties.

> Media coverage: including the sponsor in press releases and activities that receive media attention, a public relations campaign for the sponsor's market, advertising and event promotional pieces that include

sponsor material, shared ad time if there's TV coverage, event-driven promotional radio or TV, announcing the sponsorship on billboards, vehicles, public transport and through shared media.

> Audience knowledge. A property might give a sponsor access to its own audience research, or the opportunity to insert questions in its next audience survey.

> Pass-through rights allow a sponsor to pass the benefits on to a subsidiary or client company, provided the second company is also acceptable to the property.

> Speaking opportunities with the property for the sponsor's personnel.

> Social media attention.

> Brand value, exposure or sales leads within the property's clientele or audience, or hosting opportunities that are meaningful to the sponsor.

Just to prove these points, let's look for sponsorship potential at a conference or industry event. At first glance, it doesn't seem promising. The organizers don't own the building or control most of what happens inside it. Attendance may be fairly small. Delegates come from many different communities, but there are only a few from any one place. They are on site for just two or three days – and opportunities to step outside the conference venue are limited.

Not much chance for sponsorship there, you say? Think again!

On conference sponsorship

So many conferences across the country miss out on opportunities when they sell the traditional exhibitor booth or "presenting sponsor" title of a speaker or workshop. Often it is a cost recovery sponsorship where the organization is just trying to "cover the cost" of the lunch, the band or something else.

But people usually go to conferences by choice, as opposed to being forced to attend. They are related to other attendees by profession, industry, cause or mission, so they are a focused group. They pay money to attend. If I am a brand, large or small, and this audience can be served by my products, why am I not there? More important, why is the conference not reaching out to brands and showing them how the event can deliver their audience better than anyone else?

When you run a conference, do the people attending need to provide their own din-ners or are they included? If not, wouldn't nearby restaurants want to reach these people? Wouldn't the conference location want to entice attendees to host their next event at the same venue? Are there consultants out there who would want to reach this audience? If so, why aren't they sponsors?

Why merely sell booth space to sponsors when you can up-sell them to presenting a speaker, offering an exclusive reception, showcasing their products outside of an "exhibit hall" or having the rights to provide an applicable workshop or keynote address? What can the property offer outside of the conference that it owns or has access to?

As you plan your next conference, workshop or convention, look at what you really own. Determine what it is truly worth in the marketplace and then charge for it. Don't leave money on the table. Get your value and make sure your sponsors receive measurable ROI.

– Partnership Group – Sponsorship Specialists ™ blog, April 19, 2011

If you approach the task of compiling an inventory with an open, creative mind, you will create a far longer list than you expected. Your next task is to organize your list into categories so that similar assets are grouped together. Then set up a spreadsheet (or for a larger property, use software specifically designed for asset inventory).

The spreadsheet **(See Sample 1, pages 146-147 – Inventory Valuation and Costing Template)** should include a column for each of these headings:

> **Category/product -** A list of assets with similar ones grouped together, such as buildings, broadcast coverage, sponsor benefits, sponsor logos on property staff and volunteers.

> **Description -** A precise, brief explanation of each opportunity.

INVENTORY AND VALUATION

> **Value of benefit** - The market worth of each asset or benefit.

> **Projected sponsor cost per unit** - The estimated expense the sponsor will pay to activate the benefit, such as the cost of printing signs or banners. If the benefit relates to hospitality opportunities, show the sponsor costs for things like drinks and raffle tickets here. Listing the projected sponsor costs will alert the sponsor to the total budget needed: the rights fee for the opportunity of sponsorship, plus the costs of activation to make the sponsorship as effective as possible.

> **Number available** - How many of each benefit are available for sale; for example, how many performance stages are at a music festival.

> **Number sold** - How many of each benefit are actually sold.

> **Total sponsor cost** - Projected sponsor cost per unit multiplied by the number sold.

> **Gross revenue** - Total proceeds if every unit of the benefit were sold.

> **Property cost per unit** - What it costs the property to provide the asset. Free tickets, for example, mean lost sales revenue.

> **Property total cost** - Cost per unit multiplied by the number sold.

> **Net revenue** - Gross revenue minus the property total cost.

> **Eligibility** - Level of sponsorship required for the sponsor to qualify for the benefit.

You may have to negotiate some give and take between sponsor costs and event costs – who produces banners for instance. Get sponsors to pick up their own costs whenever possible. It is essential to identify every possible expense involved in the purchase and activation of a sponsorship so that there is no later misunderstanding of who should pay for what. Note that if you have to produce something anyway, like directional signage or printed tickets, you should not list it among the sponsorship-related expenses.

This list is long, but that doesn't mean it is complete. Use it to begin your own list of possible sponsor assets. Let it inspire you to look even further for something that may be entirely unique to your property. Emphasize that everything the property offers has value, and do your best to find a reasonably accurate market value for everything you offer.

> **EXERCISE**

Prepare an inventory evaluation for an event or property, preferably one with which you are familiar. For the purposes of this exercise, make up any details you do not have. List every possible asset or benefit you can think of for the property. Organize assets into product categories, and fill in a hypothetical description and number available for each. Transfer the information to the Inventory Valuation and Costing template. You will have filled in the first three columns: Category/Product, Description, Number Available.

In Chapter 2, you will learn how to value the inventory and complete your spreadsheet.

2
WHAT A PROPERTY'S ASSETS ARE WORTH TO POTENTIAL SPONSORS

Uneducated sponsorship sellers typically resort to guesswork, cost recovery, or a hunch based on hearsay about what their competitors charge. That off-the-cuff approach won't serve your future sponsors well. Nor will it lead you to all the money your property is worth. There's a much better way: using values and formulas that have been tested and accepted within the sponsorship industry. Each value and formula points to a concrete, measurable result that allows you and the sponsor to calculate a return on investment.

The following values and formulas are taken from the sponsorship practices of over 300 major corporations and 2,500 properties. The Partnership Group – Sponsorship Specialists™ uses them to establish fair market values for assets in an inventory. Despite the quantitative research and common practice behind them, they are only guidelines, and not necessarily applicable to all properties at all times. The value of assets may be more or less than illustrated here, depending on the uniqueness of the asset and the property.

These brands are extremely sophisticated. They clearly understand the importance of being involved in grassroots marketing. They understand that sponsorship is the key driver to successful local brand integration and grassroots initiatives. But to be successful, you need to know what you have to sell and what it is worth. These brands know the values of your assets. There is no fooling them.
– Partnership Group – Sponsorship Specialists ™ blog, January 3, 2012

SAMPLING OPPORTUNITIES
Sampling is a key benefit that most organizations undervalue. But most retail or branding sponsors want sampling opportunities, so it is very important to place a value on them.

Multiply the number of products being sampled by a rate of $0.05 to $0.20 per item. If the product is stuffed into a goody bag, use the lower end of the scale – at or near $0.05 per item. If face-to-face sampling is offered, you can use the higher value, but you should count only the number of people likely to receive samples, not your entire attendance.

Depending on the audience, the value will vary, and some of that variance is subjective. For instance, at a women's fashion event, a nail polish sample in a goody bag may garner more than $0.05 per item – probably $0.07 to $0.10 per item because the target audience aligns with a core purchasing demographic.

EXAMPLE:

1. A charity run expects about 5,000 people, of whom 3,000 are registered to run. The value of placing a sample in the runners' goody bag would be $150 (3000 bags x $.05 each).

2. A ski event includes 200 competitors. An estimated 1,000 other skiers will be on the hill as well during the day. A sponsor hands out samples of mitten heat packs to all skiers, participants and non-participants alike, as they stand in line for the ski lifts. The unit value of this opportunity will be greater because the sample is personally handed to the skiers. Using the high end of the scale – a sample individually distributed to each person in a target demographic – the total sampling value is $240 ($0.20 per person x 1,200 skiers).

TICKETS AND HOSPITALITY

When calculating the value of tickets included in sponsorship packages, multiply the face value of the ticket by the number of tickets. However, if the property has a track record of delivering less than 70% of its capacity, then discount the tickets appropriately. An average attendance of 60%, for example, means the ticket is worth only 60% of its face value.

EXAMPLE:

If the package includes 100 tickets with a face value of $20 each and the property has an 80% average capacity, the value of the asset is $2,000.

If the property only gets about 60% capacity then the value is $1,200 or 60% of the face value.

If at all possible, avoid printing tickets with no face value. However, if you must produce tickets without a printed face value, then use a range based on the value of benefits received from the ticket, the uniqueness of the property and the desirability of the ticket or pass.

EXAMPLE:
For a ticket or pass with no face value for a gala event, the unit value is:
> the cost of the meal
> plus any entertainment or door prizes available to all ticketed guests at no extra cost
> divided by the number of guests.

Suppose that the meal is $45, there is a band that receives a fee of $5,000, and the door prize draw has prizes worth $2,500. Three hundred guests attend. Combine the values of the band and the prizes available for all guests – $7,500.

Divide that by the number of guests attending for a value of $25. Add that to the meal to calculate the total value of the ticket: $70.

In the case of VIP passes or special accreditation, calculate the core values in the same manner. Then add a premium for the special status. The premium can range from 10% to 50% depending on the desirability of the pass or ticket.

HOSPITALITY
The use of the property's facilities for a sponsor function has great value. So does segregated sponsor space at an event location. It further associates the sponsors with the property and lets them showcase their products or host their clients and prospects.

The calculation of these assets varies depending on the facility and its regular rental rates. If standard rates exist for space usage, that value is used. If there are no standard rates, the rate for local equivalent space must be used, along with consideration for the value of the atmosphere: a theatre stage with the set still in place, the insider status of a sports team's dressing room – these features boost the value of the space beyond what its square footage and amenities would normally command.

MAILING LISTS
Note that privacy legislation in Canada and the US prohibits selling or acquiring mailing lists to use for direct or indirect purposes without the potential recipient's permission. The best approach is to include sponsor mailing pieces in

the property's mailings or emails.

The number used for valuation is the total number of mailings delivered. The value per name on the list is between $0.10 and $0.20. Use the higher value if the list is not a compilation of other lists or if the list is not available in that form anywhere else, such as an association list.

> **EXAMPLE:**
> A sponsor coupon is included in the property's monthly mailing once per year. The number of recipients on the mailing or email list receiving the coupon is 5000. The list is compiled from other lists, including donors, several event ticket buyer lists and a members list, so the valuation is set low at $0.10 per name. The value of this asset or benefit to the sponsor is $500.00 (5000 x $0.10).

SPONSOR IDENTIFICATION IN MEASURED MEDIA

Start with the full retail value of the event or property advertisements that include the sponsor identification or logo. Take 5% to 10% of that value, depending on the degree of the sponsor's exposure within the ad. For example, is the sponsor buried in a clutter of other logos, or highlighted with a mention or more visible logo? Is the sponsor featured as a presenting sponsor?

If advertising time or space is contributed as part of a media sponsorship, be cautious about using the media sponsor's initial valuation of the ads to value the exposure of other sponsors. Like the posted hotel room rate that no-one pays under normal circumstances, the value may be inflated. If the values seem high, it may be prudent to have someone call the media outlet from a private telephone and enquire about the cash cost of purchasing an equivalent package.

When you are offering or receiving "flow through" media, use the media outlet's rate card to determine value. For example, for 20 radio commercials of 30 seconds each for full use (not just an ID mention) by the sponsor, the value is that of the commercials themselves. If each commercial is worth $125, the value of that benefit package would be $2,500.

> **EXAMPLE:**
> A sponsor's logo is included in the property's TV campaign. The total campaign (bought, donated and value-in-kind TV) is worth $32,000.

This sponsor is included in one quarter of all the TV spots along with 3 other sponsor logos. What is the value of this benefit to the sponsor?

Calculation: Divide the total value of the campaign by 4 because the logos appear in only 25% of the spots, and then multiply by 10% because there are three other sponsor logos. The actual value of this benefit to the sponsor is $800.

The process is the same for broadcast coverage exposure of a sponsor's logo or identification on signage: if a sponsor's signage will appear for a total of three minutes during a broadcast of the event, the normal retail value of that TV exposure (perhaps considered as six commercials of 30 seconds) is multiplied by 5% to 10% because the signage is shown during brief camera pans.

SPONSOR IDENTIFICATION IN NON-MEASURED MEDIA

Non-measured media includes collateral such as event programmes, building guides and marketing materials, and other publications. Opportunities within non-measured media do have value, but that value varies widely depending on the audience and the community. Professional assistance can be helpful in valuing this asset category.

Here are some basic guidelines:

> If a sponsor logo appears on a property publication such as a program or handout, the valuation is $0.00325 to $0.065 per publication printed. A logo or other identification with no other logos on the front cover will garner the higher end, but very seldom more than $0.025 per printed publication. By comparison, a logo or other identification on a "sponsor page" with other sponsors' materials is valued at the low end, perhaps 1/3 of one cent or $0.00325.

> PA announcements also use the same scale of $0.00325 to $0.065 per attendee who will hear the mention or tag. A simple mention of the sponsor's name is calculated at the lower end of the scale. A name mention that includes a sell line ("Remember to stop in to Buddy's on your way home and pick up a barbecued chicken!") or is integrated into the performance in some way, such as a promotional contest or presenting

sponsor mention, will rate higher.

> A speaking opportunity will rate even higher on the scale of $0.00325 to $0.065 per attendee.

> Website exposure is typically overvalued. A logo or other identification on the sponsor page is worth $0.00325 per unique user. A logo placed in the overall website template or located on a specialized website with a targeted audience is worth between $0.00325 and $0.065 per unique user. The richest opportunity for website exposure is the chance to provide content – a featured article that includes the sponsor's logo and product descriptions.

INTANGIBLE ASSETS

Intangible assets are almost impossible to duplicate. Sometimes they are even a once-in-a-lifetime experience. Examples include the chance to meet a celebrity, an affiliation between the celebrity and the sponsor's brand, a private reception for a sponsor and guests with a celebrity, cast members or star athletes, a behind-the-scenes tour, or a unique speaking or participatory activity such as being on the players' bench, throwing the opening pitch, taking a cameo role in a production or riding in a tank.

Because they are unique, intangible assets are a challenge to value. When a property creates a customized program for a sponsor, an intangible asset may carry huge value as a key component to the sponsorship's success and a source of incremental dollars for both the sponsor and the property.

The asset's uniqueness, the number of sponsors who will have access to it, the intrinsic value to the sponsor for branding, sales or hosting and the cost of fulfillment must all be taken into account. Such assets can range in value from $500 to $100,000 or more. Imagine for a moment that you have a chance to meet Bono backstage. Instinct tells us that such an opportunity is indeed valuable – and the rarity that makes it so valuable also makes it extremely difficult to determine its market worth.

To assist you with the next exercise, refer to Sample 2, pages 148-155 – the Inventory Asset Valuation Matrix. It includes all formulas discussed in this chapter in convenient chart form.

> **EXERCISE**
> *So far, you have learned to determine what you have to sell and place a value on it. Now return to the spreadsheet on which you have listed all possible assets for the property you have chosen. Establish hypothetical numbers and demographics for your audience, set the number of each asset available, and calculate the value of your inventory. Be very conservative at valuing all your assets, especially media, so that your product will stand up under scrutiny by prospective sponsors.*
>
> *Where did you find ambiguities in the valuation process?*
> *How did you resolve them?*
>
> *What surprised you most when you calculated the value of your assets?*

REALITY CHECK – EVERY PROPERTY HAS SOMETHING TO SELL, AND USUALLY MORE TO SELL THAN YOU MIGHT THINK.

REALITY
CHECK

Don't stop with a list of obvious items like naming rights and logo placement. Think about how a sponsor might appear in or leverage every facet of your property. Then use accepted industry valuations to find out the genuine market value of every one of those opportunities.

Now you know what you have to sell and you know what it is worth. The next section on Prospecting will help you to determine who might want to buy what your property is preparing to sell.

PROSPECTING

"WE WILL NEVER ATTRACT A SPONSOR. Our profile is too low, so we need to build a brand first. Why would any business be interested in sponsoring us?"

"We're doing a great job! Look how much everyone enjoys our event!" or, "Look at our great new building/mission/programs! Company X should be glad to sponsor us. I'll make the call this afternoon and get them on board."

Of course, the truth of sponsorship lies somewhere between these extremes. Every property has something valuable to offer – but only to the right sponsor. And every business can benefit from sponsorship – but only with the right property.

Toni Ennis, a manager of marketing, advertising and events with over 20 years sponsorship experience at a national Canadian insurance company says, "Sponsorship is becoming more and more important for companies as a marketing tool. Sponsorships have to align with my business goals and my target audience. Younger workers want to see community involvement from their company."

This section on Prospecting will show you where to look for suspects (your "long list" of possible sponsors) and how to create your "short list" of prospects that are worth the time and effort of a discovery process.

REALITY CHECK

3
HOW TO FIND YOUR TOP CANDIDATE FOR A WIN-WIN SPONSORSHIP

RESEARCH YOUR AUDIENCE

The more you know about your audience, the more precisely you can determine which brands need to reach them. Distribute surveys at events and online or hire a research company to do it for you. Ask your guests about their feelings on sponsorship. Would they be comfortable accepting a corporate presence in order to improve their own experience? Find out what they like and dislike, where they shop, if they are married, whether they have children and in what age groups, whether they drink wine or beer, eat out frequently, enjoy working on their homes or gardens, if they travel, if they have pets. All this will point the way to products and services they need and want.

With a clear picture of your audience, you will be able to determine the brands that target the same demographic groups. Watch TV programs, read magazines and visit websites that are popular with your audience. Look at the advertisers – stores, financial institutions, services and specialty companies – trying to reach your audience through those media channels. Add those companies to your list for prospect research.

Pay attention to employment issues as well. As you read, you may learn about talent shortages in a particular sector or region. You may come across a story about recruitment and retention issues at a particular company. Put yourself in a recruiter's shoes and look for potential hires among your audience. Do you see the skilled workers those companies need to hire? If you do, then add the businesses to your research list.

SUSPECTS AND PROSPECTS

Inexperienced sponsorship seekers can easily fall into the trap of identifying "likely" sponsors for the wrong reasons. Something in their brand or behavior makes the company seem like a perfect fit with your organization – from your point of view. A company may be very profitable and have lots of cash available. It may even sponsor your competitors. But don't get excited – that does not make it a prospect for you. So far, it's just a suspect. Only research and careful, face-to-face questioning will establish whether it belongs on your list of prospects and why.

Companies become prospects when you begin building a relationship because you have researched their business and discovered that they align with your organization. You have something they want, something you can deliver to assist their business development.

It comes down to one thing – can you help the sponsors achieve their business goals? If you can help them, and if you can take away some hurt, you will get their money. If you can't, don't bother writing the proposal. As a sponsorship marketing specialist, the property is a solution provider. If you cannot provide solutions, don't bother pitching the offer. As a property, you are there to serve the sponsors. They are not there to serve you. It is that simple. And if you follow that premise, you will get the money.
– Partnership Group – Sponsorship Specialists™ blog, March 13, 2012

WHO IS YOUR COMPETITION?

When you consider launching a new product or service, analyzing your competitors early in the game is vital. That analysis is just as important with sponsorship – after all, sponsorship is a product or service you intend to offer in return for fair payment. In your sponsorship landscape, your competitor is anyone who can offer your sponsorship prospects a cost-effective way to meet their business objectives. You must show your prospects how you can meet their objectives more efficiently.

Prepare yourself to answer these questions:

> "Why should we consider sponsoring your property? Newspaper and billboard advertising are already doing a great job for us."

> "How can you do a better job for me than any of the other sponsorship candidates who have pitched to me?"

> "Why would sponsoring you be more effective than our Internet and social media presence?"

> "Can you deliver better results than my direct mail campaigns?"

In other words, any other channel – not just another sponsorship property, but any channel – that might help your prospects build relationships with the audience they seek is your competitor. Some of the money for sponsorship may come from budgets for other marketing initiatives such as TV ads, direct mail and social media campaigns. That's why it is so important to show prospects how sponsoring your property can be more effective than a media campaign alone.

The more you can integrate with a company's existing efforts, the more you can show how sponsoring you will improve its overall marketing results, the stronger your chances will be.

THE USUAL SUSPECTS

When inexperienced sellers look for likely sponsors, they often begin by searching for large, wealthy or high-profile companies. But size, wealth and reputation tell you nothing about the potential fit between a company's objectives and your assets. Major financial institutions, highly visible Crown companies, oil and gas players, large retail chains, telecommunications companies engaged in cutthroat competition, or industry sector leaders – any of these may be prominent in your region, but that alone will not make them your prospects. These companies are already besieged by many properties that fit their needs, and many more that knock on their door purely because they are prominent.

You can save vast amounts of time and effort through one simple strategy: seek out relationships within your network.

MAKING CONNECTIONS

You don't know any likely prospects? Think again!

> Look at what you buy or rent: banking services, office supplies, leased vehicles, office space and equipment, utilities, food, beverages and program supplies. Analyze each company on your list of suppliers. How could sponsoring you help them grow their business?

> Look at the business you already create for others – the hotel down the street from your stadium, the restaurant across from your theatre. If you know you are already growing their business, you can make a convincing pitch that they can reap even greater rewards if they invest with you.

> Involve the people who already care. Every property has donors, members, parents, families, staff, performers, a business network, audiences or stakeholders. Some will already be more closely connected –

leading donors, long-time season ticket holders, active parents. Give them another way to contribute by asking them where they work, who they know, or what companies they own. If their email addresses tell you where they work, ask them for appropriate contacts within their companies.

> Look at the people you can deliver to a sponsor. Research your audience demographics and purchasing behaviour, then approach targets that need to sell to that audience. Consider how you can enhance your event to engage more of your participants' interests and create greater sponsorship potential. For example, a music festival or an annual walk for a charitable cause might study its audience and discover that many participants own dogs. Encouraging people to bring their dogs to the event might make it an appealing sponsorship property for pet food producers and vendors.

CASE STUDY: WINNERS

Q: WOULD WINNERS BE INTERESTED IN SPONSORING YOUTH SOCCER? WHY OR WHY NOT?

A: Yes. Through careful research, the Canadian Soccer Association (Soccer Canada) deduced that women between the ages of 25 and 40 are Winners' top customer demographic. When Soccer Canada asked Winners for a discovery meeting, they were rejected with the comment, "We don't sell athletic equipment!"

As the Soccer Canada representative apologized, he casually mentioned that his "soccer moms" were women between 25 and 40. Then he hung up.

Within minutes, Winners called back with a much more cordial tone. They eventually became the title sponsor for the Canadian Soccer Association's women's and women's youth soccer. Activation tactics (see Section 5, beginning on page 83) included having the women's national soccer team visit stores to hand out soccer balls and picture cards and meet fans. When the team visited the Winners College Park store in Toronto, young fans dressed in their local team uniforms willingly lined up 90 minutes before opening time to meet their soccer heroes.

The Canadian Soccer Association's 2013 list of sponsors included other brands of interest to moms and female players – Bell (telecommunications, cable), BMO (banking), Garnier (hair and skin care), Mark's (casual clothing) and Ombrelle (skin care). Winners now understands that the key to effective sponsorship lies in a holistic understanding of the audience that a property provides.

EXAMPLE:

The Canadian Western Agribition once focused its sponsorship efforts only on brands that marketed directly to its farmer participants, for example, farm equipment and feed companies. After analyzing not just its participants but its audience, the Agribition began reaching out to other brands, pitching the full range of consumer needs among its rural participants and urban fairgoers.

Sponsors in 2013 included Budweiser, SaskTel, BMO, Saskatchewan Credit Unions, CIBC, RBC, TD Canada Trust, Ramada, Coca-Cola and the Saskatchewan Arts Board.

CASE STUDY: TORONTO SYMPHONY ORCHESTRA

What might a sponsorship between the Toronto Symphony Orchestra and Banana Republic look like? The orchestra needs to attract younger people to its audience and ultimately to its subscriber base. Banana Republic needs to increase store traffic. Its key customer demographic is females aged 14 to 24.

HOW THEY DID IT: The TSO planned a four-concert subscription series featuring hip-hop music geared to Banana Republic's target market. The players wore Banana Republic clothing instead of their usual tuxedos and black dresses. Live models in Banana Republic clothing distributed coupons to audience members. Coupons were valid for just two weeks after the concert date.

DID IT WORK? Yes. The first concert sold only 50% of its available seats. But it was such a hit with the audience that a buzz developed. Banana Republic leveraged that word of mouth with in-store promotional marketing and point-of-sale materials about the concert. The remaining three concerts sold out as a package, not as single tickets. Banana Republic saw double-digit increases in both store traffic and sales in the two-week period after the second, third and fourth concerts.

*"Our sponsors often want recruitment and retention objectives to be met, especially in boom cycles. They want to reach the graduates of programs that align with their needs." – **Lisa Marie Didow**, formerly MacEwan University*

RESEARCH YOUR SUSPECTS

How do you determine what your suspects want? Start by following business trends. Media reports, your competitor's sponsors, and product placement or sampling programs by particular brands may give you ideas. But even then, though these companies may seem likely, they are only suspects until you do more research to find a possible fit between their marketing goals and your opportunities.

Newspapers and blogs are helpful sources for both trends and details on business developments. Is a company expanding into new regions or opening new outlets? Is it taking over another corporation? What does it sponsor now, and what does that tell you about its business goals, the audience it needs and the activation tactics it prefers? (Or is their activation lacking? If so, that's an opportunity for you!) Is one company mounting a concerted PR campaign or attracting favorable media attention? If so, can you help its competitors boost their public profile?

Corporate online presence is another source of helpful information. Follow your top suspects on Twitter, like them on Facebook, see if you can connect with them or some of their people through LinkedIn. Analyze what you find on their websites and through search engines. Pay attention to the key businesses in the sectors you're targeting – not just the suspect companies, but their suppliers, distributors and purchasers.

A word of caution here: Your research will give you essential background material. Used properly, it will help you ask deeper, more intelligent questions in your discovery sessions. (You will learn more about that in Section 3, p. 35.) But the research will not reveal the full story about a company's marketing challenges, for instance, or the impact of its high staff turnover on its profitability. Only a staff member who trusts your discretion and commitment to helping the company will share that insider information.

WHO MAKES SPONSORSHIP DECISIONS?

When you seek a meeting, find out who makes the sponsorship decisions. If the company is small, you might even begin by asking to see the president, CEO or owner. You will probably be referred to someone else, someone who may or may not be the decision-maker. That does not mean you will fail. It is simply how that particular company organizes its responsibilities, and says nothing about how the company views you or your chances of success.

With over 25 years of experience, I only get to the decision-maker about half the time. You can still succeed. The important thing is to be sure that the person can give you the information you want during the discovery interviews, and will be your champion if the two of you decide that your property might be a good fit with the company's sponsorship needs.
*– **Brent Barootes**, Partnership Group – Sponsorship Specialists™ prospecting workshop.*

In a larger company, you may find yourself meeting with someone whose involvement in sponsorship is superficial. As the prospect's needs and your ability to meet them become clearer, you may have to interview and influence more than one person. Turn that into an asset! In a complex organization, the more people who hear about how they could benefit from a sponsorship with you, the better your chances will be.

Target the right people for what you have to offer, and tailor your questions to the people you have the opportunity to meet. Someone in marketing will describe one portion of the corporate picture, but a peer in the community investment department will have different information and a very different perspective. The human resources VP will want to talk about tying sponsorship to staff recruitment and retention. The sales VP will be more interested in the direct business you can offer – housing for visiting artists or an army of volunteers, a sports team's bank account. Keep asking questions – often the same questions – with every new person you meet.

When there are several corporate divisions, you may have to convince multiple division managers or marketers – but your prize may be much bigger. For example, Toshiba Canada makes laptop computers, AV equipment and MRI machines as well as photocopiers. All three product divisions joined in sponsoring the 2005 Canada Summer Games in Regina Saskatchewan for an investment of $1.2 million.

If you are directed to the donations committee, an advertising manager, or the company's public relations agency, you may have to educate them about sponsorship as well as investigating the company and its needs. That will also be true if you begin with the procurement officer of one of your suppliers.

A company with a healthy sponsorship strategy, on the other hand, may have a sponsorship director who is well-informed about strategies, implementation and evaluation of sponsorships, and is keen to explore a fit between corporate objectives and your audience.

KNOWING THE DECISION-MAKER

Even if you are never able to meet the sponsorship decision-maker, a little research will tell you a lot about how to frame your approach and even your proposal if you submit one. A recent study of corporate managers found that they travel 60% to 70% of the time. On an average day, they –

> receive 120 to 150 emails;
> read and perhaps return only 25 to 40 of those;
> receive approximately 20 phone calls; and
> return just four to eight of those.

Now add to that the typical manager's attendance of six to ten meetings or teleconferences weekly, and the use of 3,000 to 4,000 wireless and data minutes each month. (Cynthia Beiler, U.S. Cellular, 2009)

Does that picture of your decision-maker's working life help you understand why you are not likely to have your calls and emails returned? Don't let that stop you! Find a likely champion from the people you are able to meet, then determine what other departments are also applicable, starting with the one that seems like the best fit. Through it all, make sure your champion understands your property's potential, believes in it, and will make sure that your enquiries (and eventually your proposal, if appropriate) continue moving through the corporate chain.

> **EXERCISE**
> *Choose an event, a sports team, a municipal facility or a public sector building to be your hypothetical sponsorship property. Prepare a list of prospects for that property. Determine the rationale for your list. What is the fit between the property and each prospect? Be prepared to justify your list based on what you know about the company. Leave money out of the discussion for now. Focus on who qualifies as a sound prospect for this property and why.*

REALITY CHECK – THERE IS AT LEAST ONE APPROPRIATE SPONSOR FOR EVERY PROPERTY.

However, you will only identify likely candidates by setting aside your preconceptions about your audience, users or members, and about the small and large companies you think you know.

Analyze and understand the people you attract then, analyze and understand your suspects. Finally, based on sound evidence uncovered during your research, bring your most likely suspects into your "prospect pipeline" and begin asking for meetings.

In the next section – Discovery – you'll learn what to ask, what to listen for, and when to talk (hint: not often, especially about your property).

DISCOVERY

IMAGINE A YOUNG WOMAN ENTERING A CAR DEALERSHIP with two young children in tow. Immediately a salesman approaches and launches into a sales pitch for the newest minivans. He stresses the cargo capacity, the rear seat DVD screens, and the many child safety features that benefit her and her presumed young family.

But the young woman isn't the mother of those children. She is their youngest aunt, and the children are on a rare visit from their home in another province. She is also a successful investment banker looking for a sports car to celebrate her promotion. She leaves to find a dealer that will take time to listen to her needs – or even better, ask what her needs are.

Assumptions kill sales. Discovery sessions are essential because they equip you to explore sponsorship based on facts, not assumptions.

– Partnership Group – Sponsorship Specialists™ Discovery Workshop

4
MAKING DISCOVERY SESSIONS WORK FOR YOU

A discovery session is an introductory meeting (or sometimes a series of meetings). Somewhat like a first date, it allows you to assess compatibility. You want to learn about the company's goals, objectives and desires, but also about their challenges. Where do they hurt? Do they have an employee attrition issue? Lead generation challenges? Public relations setbacks? How can you take the hurt away?

The one thing you must never do in a discovery meeting is pitch what you have to offer – even though your instincts, your sales training and your boss all tell you otherwise. You are not there to sell, or even to tell. Your only job is to listen to the prospect. You must focus on what the prospect needs, not what you have to offer. To make sure that the conversation stays on the topic of the prospect's needs, go in empty-handed. Take nothing, not even a simple brochure about your amazing mission or your dynamite event. Listen. Take notes. If it seems that the exploration might continue, send a tailored, one-page document the following week after immediately sending a thank-you note (preferably handwritten).

Now you have three touch points: the initial meeting, the thank-you note, and the follow-up document. Your relationship has begun.

Discovery meetings are absolutely vital to your success. There may be several over time as business objectives shift, people leave or change roles or departments are integrated with others. In Canada, moving from prospect qualification to closing generally takes 18 to 22 months, although there are exceptions, both shorter and longer.

The time needed to arrange sponsorships can vary wildly outside the usual 18- to 22-month period. When Fire Within finally secured its first meeting with prospect EnCana, the meeting was booked for just 30 minutes. It went on for three hours as ideas developed and grew. At the end of the meeting, EnCana asked for a price, Fire Within asked for $300K, and the deal was done.

At the other end of the scale, a sponsorship process that starts out looking easy can turn out to be very lengthy indeed. When SaskTel, a provincial Crown corporation, signed on as a sponsor of the Canada Games, it knew it would have to be there. There was no way the Government of Saskatchewan, which was on the hook for

any revenue shortfalls but no sponsorship recognition, would allow competitors like Rogers, Bell or TELUS be the "official supplier of communications services" in their province. Despite that, the signed agreement took two years to secure, even after a verbal commitment.
– Partnership Group – Sponsorship Specialists™ Discovery workshop, Toronto, 2013

Most sponsorship sellers walk into a first meeting and begin pitching. A prospect might actually be dumbfounded when you structure a meeting that is focused on helping them rather than pitching to them. At the end of the meeting or series of meetings, you want to leave with enough information to build a custom proposal that addresses their unique needs and demonstrates how your inventory of benefits will deliver the results the prospect wants.

Although the prospecting and discovery process takes time, deals that begin this way are closed at a much higher rate than when proposals are built on assumptions and high hopes. Both parties find the sponsorships more effective when they build a relationship along the way. The sponsorship becomes a genuine partnership rather than a supplier service agreement.

5
MAKING THE MEETING OR MEETINGS WORK

Do they have something unique to offer that truly engages our target audience? Is there a clear engagement plan? I want to see that they've done their research on fit and the common qualities we share. I'll also take a meeting if it's a referral from someone else that we've worked with and trust.
– **Angela Saveraux**, *Canadian Western Bank*

I see more properties than many people do. It's a mistake on our side of the fence not to learn about organizations. It's the potential for partnership that gets me excited – when I see that they're interested in helping me as much as I help them. I want to see a focus on the relationship, not the transaction.
– **Ron Podbielski**, *formerly Farm Credit Canada, SaskEnergy and SaskTel*

HOW TO GET THE MEETING

Calling someone you do not know to ask for a meeting can be a daunting task. But if you go in without looking for opportunities to sell, you will be amazed by how much information people are willing to share. These preparatory steps will help to build your confidence and focus on your goal rather than your anxiety.

> Make sure you call the right person (or people) for your purpose. Your research should tell you whether you are targeting the CEO, the sales vice-president, the community investment person, the human resources director, or someone else. If you can see a good reason to involve more than one person from the start, do your best to set a meeting with all of them.

> Know in advance if there are gatekeepers between you and the person you should see. Research them as carefully as you would your target person. If you build a relationship with them, they can be among your allies and champions. If you are unable to build an alliance with them, then move on. Call at a time when you suspect your target person is in the office but the gatekeeper is not, such as early mornings or late evenings.

> Know that you will offer the most convenient time and place for your prospect. Some research indicates that Friday is the best day for meet-

ings. People are in a positive frame of mind, they are unlikely to be distracted by an emerging crisis, and they have the entire weekend to think about your discussion. Most people appreciate the time saved by meeting in their office, and you will have the chance to observe the company atmosphere and perhaps build bridges with the receptionist. Stay flexible; some may prefer a breakfast, lunch or coffee offsite.

> Remind your target of the connection – that you have a person or organization in common, or that you have noticed their current sponsorships and believe you have something better to offer.

> Emphasize from the beginning that you will walk in empty-handed – no proposals, no pitches – because you are coming to listen, not to sell. In many cases, your prospect will relax right away.

> When you ask for a meeting, your only goal is to get the meeting. If your prospect brushes you off with comments like "I've done that and it doesn't work" or "I have no budget," don't attempt to address them. Instead, focus on getting the meeting to help their business grow, not pitch a proposal. Name a day and time. That will switch your prospect's focus from whether they want to meet to whether they are available that day. Watch for any sense that your target's irritation is building – if so, give in gracefully.

*"Properties don't always have the most up-to-date information available to them when using research tools like a potential sponsor's website. We do some things differently from region to region – that's an example of the kind of thing you only learn in the discovery session. I help them tweak their application to reflect regional tactics." – **Angela Saveraux**, Canadian Western Bank*

"Often brands want to boost the objectives that they're not good at rather than what you've noticed them doing. So don't make assumptions based on what they already do well. . . . I try for one discovery session a week. I want their brand to add to my customer's experience. That's what I'm looking for. I want a brand profile with a cutting-edge, fashionable image and a large following. I want to walk away from a discovery session thinking, 'My customers are going to love this!'"
*– **Daniel Person**, West Edmonton Mall*

"Corporations are interested in the goodwill of the branding connection that comes with partnering with World Vision. However, in our experience, their top goals have been to increase sales and to boost their social media presence."
– **Neil Parekh**, *World Vision*

AT THE MEETING

When you arrive at the meeting, you should already have clarified the sponsorship roles of the person or people you will meet. Are they initiators who will propose the sponsorship internally? Influencers who will recommend or discourage it? Decision-makers with financial accountability? Executives who might overrule the decision-makers? Or are they users – the staff who will implement and leverage the sponsorship? Knowing each person's role will help you frame your questions and keep your expectations realistic.

In your introduction, your first comment should be "Thank you for meeting with me." Remind them you are there to learn and not to pitch. Do not talk about your property unless they ask for detail. Ask for permission to take notes.

Then remind them of the connection you have previously established – the person you know in common, the signage or other sponsorships you have noticed, your experience using their products, the role of your key volunteer or board member who is on the company's staff.

"It's easy to speculate, to make assumptions about what corporations want, especially if you do a whole lot of research about what they're already doing. But we don't know what we don't know. Go into the discovery session with a clean slate, without being influenced by a lot of research. It's easy to speculate about the value of goodwill from the brand recognition. But it's the discovery session that confirms whether brand recognition is important to the prospect."
– **Neil Parekh**, *World Vision*

"Different companies have different needs. Companies link sponsorships to what they're trying to achieve as a business. I've worked for companies in three sectors – they all had different sponsorship goals. For the telecommunications company, it was all about bodies and impressions. The utility wanted sponsorships that positioned it as a good corporate citizen. And unlike the other two, the agricultural credit corporation wanted properties with a rural focus, not an urban one."
– **Ron Podbielski**, *formerly Farm Credit Canada, SaskEnergy and SaskTel*

A major oil and gas corporation sponsored the young audience series for a city theatre. Through careful questioning in the discovery stage, the theatre's sponsorship manager learned that the company didn't want a big profile. Rather, they wanted to let 20-somethings and 30-somethings know that they were interested in them because many of the company's staff are in that age group.

GETTING THE INFORMATION YOU NEED

After your introduction, begin asking questions like these:

1. What is your business? Make sure you understand it fully. Even after research, you may not be aware of all the company's products, services, or the regions in which it operates.

2. What aspects of your business are most important for your success – for example, guaranteed delivery time, group sales, product awareness, brand penetration?

3. In your other sponsorships, what do you like best? What do you dislike most? What other sponsorships do you do? How do you feel about them?

4. What would you like from a sponsorship? If you could create one from the beginning, what might it look like? What would you change about other sponsorships you have done? Prompt them with ideas until they have created their ideal scenario.

5. Do you have particular objectives for your sponsorships, such as generating leads, driving store traffic, engaging staff, bolstering image, generating recruitment leads or building your brand? With this question, you are really asking "Where do you hurt – what needs to work better for your business to be more successful?"

6. What are you doing to meet those objectives now – advertising, hosting opportunities, direct mail, multi-level marketing, buying lists, providing better service, offering great staff benefits, developing in-house talent, other?

7. How do you measure the success of a sponsorship? How do you make

certain that the results are due to the sponsorship and not to a coincidental factor or another marketing initiative?

8. Where do make your profit? A car dealer makes most of its profits from its service department, not from car sales. For a pizza chain, group sales on off-nights may be more profitable than individual orders at peak times.

9. What can you tell me about your sponsorship budgets, both cash and value in kind? What is your overall marketing budget? How does it break down among direct mail, print, sampling and other tactics? (This question encourages the company to tap into other budgets besides the line item labelled "sponsorship.")

10. Who is your competition? Competition for a soft drink maker includes all beverages, not just other soft drink brands. Knowing the full range of competitors will build your understanding of your prospect's business – and also gives you other companies you might add to your prospect list.

11. What is your competitive advantage? Why would a consumer or client buy from you rather than your competitor?

12. What is sponsorship for you? Is it a marketing tool, a way to support the community, a straightforward donation, a hosting opportunity, a place to showcase your product, or something else?

13. What is your fiscal year? When do you prepare budgets? Could you go outside your budget if the sponsorship is just right for you? Could you tap funds from other departments or programs?

14. If I were to bring you a suitable proposal, who would make the decision to accept or reject it? If the decision-makers are not at your meeting, ask whether you would have a chance to present to them at the right time. If not, then who would meet with you about a proposal? How many people must review and approve it? Is the decision made locally? If the people in the room cannot make the decision, can they champion it?

The City of Toronto sought sponsorship for its Livegreen Toronto Festival promoting environmentally sustainable lifestyles. At a discovery meeting with Canadian Tire, the city's sponsorship staff learned that Canadian Tire planned to launch its own environmental initiative, "Blue Planet." Tactics included a $25 discount coupon for customers who brought in their old gasoline mower and purchased a new push mower or an energy-efficient electric one. Canadian Tire planned to distribute those coupons by direct mail.

The city persuaded Canadian Tire to move Blue Planet's direct mail budget into its sponsorship of Livegreen Toronto by pointing out that some of the direct mail would be wasted on apartment distribution. Instead, the city inserted the coupons into homeowners' water bills. The coupon distribution reached the target demographic more effectively because people with houses usually have lawns. It also associated the city's own name and brand with Canadian Tire's lawnmowers.

Blue Planet's marketing budget included radio spots. The City of Toronto had a massive media budget for Livegreen, and invited Canadian Tire to contribute some of its own marketing budget so that the two partners together could create greater media impact. The higher amount allowed them to set up a remote broadcast related to Livegreen in each of the 19 Canadian Tire franchises in Toronto.
*– **Brent Barootes**, Discovery Session Workshop, June 2013*

With every question, dig deeper for more detailed information if you can. You will be surprised how much information your prospects will give you once they learn you are there to help them, not to sell them something. Keep the questions focused on your prospect and the answer to their most important question – "What's in it for me?"

"Above all, I'm looking for a good fit. Curling events fit for us. They usually have a beer garden, so our traffic safety messages make sense in that context. It's also an audience that buys property insurance, so it makes sense for both our business lines."
*– **Toni Ennis**, the manager of marketing, advertising and events for a national Canadian insurance company.*

CLOSING THE MEETING
Whether the meeting is the first one in the discovery process or the final one, never leave without setting a date for the next meeting. At each meeting, keep to the ending time that was originally set. A single meeting rarely brings you to the

point where you should ask if the company would consider looking at a proposal. Instead, you will almost always find that the time is up well before you have everything you need.

As you move to close a discovery meeting, your prospects may start asking questions about your sponsorship expectations. If they ask how much money you're looking for, you can say that you don't have a figure in mind because you came to learn, not to sell.

Finally, when you have had enough meetings to be fully informed, give an example of the fit that you see between the prospect's needs and what you have to offer, for example, "We can deliver the 18-34 female demographic you need both on site by sampling and experiential opportunities, and through our newsletters and website."

Notice the language that prospects use during the discovery conversations. If they consistently use "partnership" rather than "sponsorship" or emphasize that the company sells "memories" or "status" rather than product features, use the same language in your responses.

Next, review the budget range that you believe you have determined during the interviews. Say something like, "If I were to prepare a proposal based on our discussions, would I be correct in building two options for your review, with one in the $15,000 to $25,000 range and a second at our category exclusivity level of $50,000 to $75,000?"

Know your clients' timelines for decision making. Even if their deadline is far off, you must still create a sense of urgency. Set timelines for steps toward the close so you can move the process forward. Failure to achieve small wins along this long road will cause you to be left out of the decision-making process.
– Partnership Group – Sponsorship Specialists ™ blog, February 7, 2012

If your prospects encourage you to submit, check the timeline and their willingness to be available for further information during the preparation. Invite them to experience the property in the meantime, perhaps by receiving your newsletter, attending a smaller event, or receiving advance news as event details are settled, new team players are signed, or speakers and entertainers are booked. Emphasize that you want to build a partnership that benefits everyone. Ask if you may add them to appropriate mailing and email lists.

Finally, secure the date for the meeting to review the proposal and the deadline to submit the proposal beforehand.

When you listen to prospects and build proposals based around what they need in the right budget range, you will succeed. When you think you know what the client needs or are trying to "sell to close a deal," you will most likely fail. Unless you have gone through discovery after discovery and learned all the information you can, you should not pitch a proposal.

Don't take shortcuts. Generally it is unwise to write up a proposal after two discovery sessions, let alone one. Follow up. Clarify what you learned. Learn some more. Get to know in detail what the prospect is seeking. Ensure the budget is right. Then pitch and close. – Partnership Group – Sponsorship Specialists ™ blog, September 20, 2011

> **EXERCISE**
> *Think of the company you know best, perhaps your employer or your favorite business. What should a property know about it before submitting a proposal? Identify one property that would be suitable for this company to sponsor, and justify your choice.*

TO SUM UP

The best sponsorships, like the best marriages, happen when each partner truly understands the other. Discovery is the dating stage of the relationship you hope to build. Your role is to ask the right questions, then listen, listen and listen some more as your prospects reveal their hopes and needs. Be prepared to set up as many "dates" or discovery sessions as it takes to get the information you need. When your prospects see that your goal is listening, not selling, they will happily tell you what you want to know.

It takes patience to persist through a full discovery process. Keep asking questions, keep reiterating that you are asking for meetings so you can learn, not so you can sell, and close each meeting with an agreement about the next step you will take together. When you are fully informed, you will be able to ask whether a proposal that engages a certain demographic and falls into a particular budget range would be suitable.

If you have done your discovery properly, the answer will be "yes."

PROPOSALS

REALITY CHECK – AS A PROPERTY, YOU ARE THERE TO SERVE THE SPONSORS. THEY ARE NOT THERE TO SERVE YOU.

REALITY
CHECK

Can you help the sponsors achieve their business goals? If you can help them, and if you can take away some hurt, you will get the money. If you can't, don't bother writing the proposal. As a sponsorship marketing specialist, the property is basically a "solution provider." If you cannot provide solutions, don't bother pitching the offer. As a property, you are there to serve the sponsors. They are not there to serve you. It is that simple. And if you follow that premise, you will get the money.
– Partnership Group – Sponsorship Specialists ™ blog, March 13, 2012

Traditionally, proposals from properties have had three things in common:

1. Assets are packaged in levels, usually called something like "Gold," "Silver" and "Bronze." A progressively lower price and smaller list of benefits applies to each level. The list sends the message that the pre-packaged amounts, designations and benefits are the only available combinations.

2. They are printed by the dozen or even by the hundred on the most impressive stock the property can afford.

3. Without prior contact, they are distributed with a form letter to previous sponsors, possible sponsors and complete unknowns.

Does any of this make sense? No!

In this section you will learn a completely different, customized approach that results in a unique proposal for each prospect. With this method, the proposal for Company A reflects everything you learned in the research and discovery stages. It presents a customized list of assets and benefits and ties them directly to

Company A's business objectives. It prices the sponsorship in accordance with a budget figure that Company A has already indicated to be comfortable.

Under no circumstances is that same proposal appropriate for its competitor, Company B, even when the two companies sell the same products to the same markets in the same regions.

6
WHY CUSTOM PROPOSALS ARE BEST FOR PROPERTIES AND BUYERS

This brief comparison of traditional and custom proposals will help you understand how your custom proposal will differ from the cookie-cutter packages you may have seen previously.

TRADITIONAL PROPOSAL	CUSTOM PROPOSAL
Handshake and try to recall later	Every detail in writing with signatures from both parties
Document about you and why you need money	Document about the sponsor and how you can help the sponsor meet business objectives
A warm and fuzzy appeal	A concrete, objective description of benefits and costs
Letter or email of agreement with no individualized content	An extended description of every aspect of the sponsorship, concluding with a signature page
Donation letter	A sales document focused on the sponsor's needs
Addendum to a supplier agreement	A separate agreement documenting partnership even if the sponsor is also a supplier
Stock produced glossy package with folder	A simple package that contains everything necessary, clearly presented, with no irrelevant material
Gold, silver and bronze packages	A one-of-a-kind document that specifies all the assets and benefits of most use to the sponsor that are available for that sponsor's budget and not already sold to a higher-level sponsor
Direct mail or email blitz version	An individualized version prepared after extensive research and discovery

It is possible to economize somewhat with proposals. Regardless of your resources, templates can and should be prepared for parts of the proposal and used along with customized sections. You might have partial templates for different business sectors, different prospect relationships (business to business or business to consumer) or different prospect objectives such as branding, recruitment or image improvement. Of course, you will review your template for any detail that can be customized to speak to an individual prospect.

Proposals need not be beautifully printed and packaged with high-quality stationery and folders, but never sacrifice clarity of presentation, a description of your commitment to a true partnership or the focus on how you will help prospects meet each business objective they have shared with you.

A proposal with those essential elements will stand out far above the stacks of glossy, mass- produced folders that clog the desks of corporate sponsorship officers.

If the property's resources are too limited for a fully customized approach or the sponsorship amounts are quite modest, it may not be possible or worthwhile to prepare entirely unique proposals for each prospect ready to receive one. In such scenarios, as a last resort, you may use traditional approaches or stock packages.

"Sponsorships go wrong when one or both parties don't put enough time into it to make sure it's more than just a cash transaction. We have to differentiate ourselves by doing the business side of sponsorship right and growing the human relationship. There are a million great causes out there that companies could support, so we have to create a remarkable experience for our sponsors."
– **Sue Keating**, *Youth Empowerment and Support Services*

Whether your budget for research, discovery and proposals is slender or sufficient, individualized custom proposals are just as good for you as for your prospects. Once you know each prospect's business objective, you can avoid giving away benefits that are of no use to the prospect just because they are part of "the gold package." You will also save time by not trying to sell them things they do not need.

"I'm a bank. Don't give me a proposal that offers sampling opportunities! What am I going to do? Give away $5 bills?"
– **Justine Fedak**, *BMO Financial Group, North America (BMO Harris Bank)*

PROPOSALS

WHY PROPERTIES AND BUYERS NEED PROPOSALS

In simple terms, a proposal does three things:

> It summarizes everything that the property learned by listening keenly and asking probing questions during the discovery stage.

> It lists all the benefits, rights and assets that the property wants to offer the prospect, explains how each one fits with the prospect's business goals, and specifies the investment required from the prospect to acquire those rights or assets.

> It serves as the blueprint for fulfillment and activation.

The advantages of having a record of these business arrangements are evident. But even when the property and sponsor have a long-standing relationship and are repeating a previous success, there are other, less obvious reasons to make sure that a written proposal is submitted and signed off.

A signed proposal makes the deal concrete. It can help to sell the project to a new decision-maker, allow a new staff person to pick up existing commitments quickly, or engage the interest of other departments that may benefit from leveraging the sponsorship. It can include a contract, or even be written in such a way that it becomes the legal contract.

The proposal also serves as a blueprint for tracking activation and fulfillment: what the sponsor receives, who delivers, who follows up, who pays for what, and due dates for all tasks and goods. Most sponsorship programs fail because of fulfillment. Either the sponsor fails to activate or the property fails to deliver its promised benefits. Tracking fulfillment against the terms of the proposal is essential for success.

At a higher level, the proposal describes the partnership the property would like to build with the prospect. The property's commitment to treating the sponsor as a valued partner and not as a transaction-focused supplier should shine through in every section. The proposal describes everything each partner will do for the other. It is a tremendous opportunity to explain why your property is the ideal partner for the prospect.

Proposals should not be submitted until the property has done enough discovery work to determine exactly what the prospect needs and what the budget is for both rights fees and activation. If you are not sure whether a prospect would say yes to you, it is a sign that you have not yet learned enough about the prospect.

EXAMPLE:

A property kept presenting proposals but could not close the deals. The Partnership Group – Sponsorship Specialists™ was brought in to find out why. When we slowed down the process, we discovered the issues. The property's representative was moving too fast. She was not gathering enough information to build a proposal that would close. She had not listened well. She did not know the prospect's complete objectives. In most cases, she had only done one or two discovery sessions and then felt she knew everything she needed to in order to write a proposal. She was wrong, and it showed.

The second thing was that the sponsors were not listening, or perhaps they were listening but not processing. In several cases they had actually "tuned out" information. Several of the property's proposals were rejected because of the investment level, yet the property's representative kept saying, "I talked about the investment level. I told them exactly what it would cost."

Well, let's face reality. People hear what they want to hear and have a selective memory. Repetition is critical. If the investment is going to be "about $25,000," you need to repeat that about four to five times during your discovery session, then follow up in writing. Repeat what you discussed and set out the dollar figure in print long before you build a proposal. – Partnership Group – Sponsorship Specialists™ Tuesday Morning Commentary, November 1, 2011

The importance of customized proposals cannot be emphasized too much. When brands were surveyed about their top peeves and disappointments with sponsorship, the practice of cookie-cutter "gold, silver and bronze" sponsorship approaches ranked #1. (*2012 Canadian Sponsorship Landscape Study*)

7
WHAT TO INCLUDE:
COVER PAGE; TABLE OF CONTENTS;
ABOUT THE SPONSOR; ABOUT YOU

COVER PAGE AND TABLE OF CONTENTS

A cover page need not be professionally designed to be effective. It must, though, contain a few basic items of information: logos (yours and your prospect's), the proposal's title, the name of the person to whom it was presented (not just the company or department), your name, and the date on which it was presented.

The date presented is more important than you might think. Securing sponsorships takes time, and even though you should be fairly certain of success before you present a proposal, it may still take a year or more before the deal comes to fruition. When the time lag is significant, having a date on the proposal gives you some leeway to re-examine terms and prices if your values truly have changed.

The table of contents is also a very basic page. List everything you have included. Be sure to use page numbers for easy reference, and keep the format neat and clean. As with the title page, your objective should be to present basic information quickly without slowing down the reader.

Some proposals include an executive summary if the proposal itself is long or complex. As with every other aspect of the process, take your lead from your prospect. Ask if you should include an executive summary for their reference or their manager's convenience.

ABOUT THE SPONSOR

Put the amount up front, introduced by a phrase like, "As we discussed at the meeting of June 18, you asked me for a proposal in the range of $25,000."

This section describes what the property has learned about the prospect's needs and objectives during the discovery. It should not be a summary. Instead, prove your interest and responsiveness by describing the background information and each objective as specifically as you can. Take as many pages as you need. That will help to build a convincing case a few pages later when you demonstrate how each benefit in your offer helps the prospect achieve a specific objective.

CASE STUDY: COCA-COLA AND PEPSI

How might the business objectives of Coke and Pepsi differ within a specific regional market such as southern Saskatchewan?

WHAT HAPPENED: The 2005 Canada Summer Games took place in Regina. At the time, Coca-Cola had already built huge brand recognition and garnered a market share of 80% in southern Saskatchewan. It did not need to boost brand recognition. But to grow market share even more, it wanted to influence purchasing decisions in a key demographic at a specific moment. It wanted to position itself to teens and tweens when they went to convenience stores at lunch or after school. However, corporations were barred from advertising in the region's schools.

Pepsi, by contrast, trailed Coke with a market share of just 20%. It was still at the brand-building stage, and valued high amounts of signage to reinforce its brand with restaurants and universities. Though the consumer sees "the same product" – a cola – each brand had very different objectives. If you had built proposals for both based on Coke's information, Pepsi would have had zero interest in your offer.

A successful proposal for Coke would be completely different from a proposal for Pepsi. Signage and banners –staples of the sponsorship benefits list – had huge value for Pepsi but almost none for Coke. Never assume that apparently similar corporations competing for the same market have the same needs.

In the end, each received a tailored proposal for about $500,000 in sponsorship investment. They looked nothing alike, but each proposal presented assets that would help the companies achieve their goals and each offered over the $500,000 asking price in value. Ultimately Coke became the partner. A downsized version that specifically met Coke's marketing and business objectives was signed and implemented for an investment of about $300,000 in cash, value in kind that offset specific budget items, plus additional value in kind support including products.

The recap of the prospect's needs should be as long as necessary to state every-thing you found out in discovery. If you had seven discovery meetings with the prospect, you should have a lot of information! Include it all. Make it concise, of course – it will be tedious to read otherwise – but include it all. Bullet points and numbers are acceptable and concise.

Now is the time to show that you understood the inside information that was shared during the discovery session. Most of the information companies share face to face is not on their website –

> "We care about youth" in a community responsibility report might become "We care about youth activities because it gets their parents on our side" in a discovery session.

> A petroleum or mineral exploration company might value anything that helps to resolve land use disputes, but you will not learn that with-out a candid discovery session.

> A bank's website will not say that it wants to build shareholder value. But that is a mandate for every publicly traded company, so it plays a role in sponsorship decisions.

Including such information proves you were listening and not wasting the prospect's time during those discovery meetings. It demonstrates that you under-stand them better than your competitors do.

EXAMPLE:

Thank you again for taking the time to meet with us on Thursday, June 30. From that discussion, we have worked on an initial sponsorship program to meet the specific goals and objectives of Big Business Retail Conglomerate in Canada.

Please note that this is a draft concept that will need to be fine tuned to specifically meet your needs. It may include elements that you do not feel are necessary or important. As well, there may be other ideas and concepts that we can develop to specifically meet your needs.

Big Business Retail Conglomerate in Canada:

During initial exploratory and discovery meetings we learned the following about the interests and objectives of Big Business Retail Conglomerate in Canada:

> Big Business Retail Conglomerate was started by George Billionaire in the USA. George and his family are very philanthropic. Big Business Retail Conglomerate in the U.S. is involved with the United Way, Susan G. Komen for the Cure and the BP Ride for MS.

> Big Business Retail Conglomerate Canada has been in operation over 60 years. Currently, Big Business Retail Conglomerate has 5700 corporate and franchised dollar stores across Canada.

> Big Business Retail Conglomerate owns two brands: Big Dollar Stores and Bargain Dollar Centre.

> 86% of Big Business Retail Conglomerate's business comes from women consumers. Big Business Retail Conglomerate is looking for opportunities to continue to engage with this target market, which is moms aged 40+ with kids, middle to low income, and looking for savings.

> Big Business Retail Conglomerate wants to grow its business within the western Canada market, as well as the under 35/youth market and male demographic.

> Big Business Retail Conglomerate's tagline is "Just a Dollar To Save Big" for the Big Dollar Store brand and "Everything a Bargain for $1 or Less" for the Bargain Dollar Centre brand.

> The company's overarching goal is to drive repeat and new traffic directly to the stores through brand awareness, location awareness and price.

> Big Business Retail Conglomerate sees significant value in sponsorships with experiential marketing activities that motivate participants to learn more about their stores and come to shop. They also want customers to feel good about shopping at their stores because the property means

something to them.

> Big Business Retail Conglomerate currently has sponsorships in Canada with lacrosse at local amateur and professional levels, food banks locally and regionally (nothing national), school reading programs, new Canadian immigrant societies and local community groups.

> Big Business Retail Conglomerate appreciates opportunities that drive traffic, build name and brand awareness, and build a favorable image in the community by supporting organizations such as food banks.

> The brand used in a sponsorship (Big Dollar versus Bargain Dollar) is the one in the sponsorship's market region. Where both exist the company may choose to include two brands as "competition" within a property.

> Big Business Retail Conglomerate is considering creating ways for consumers to shop online at their stores.

> Big Business Retail Conglomerate's busiest times are May/June, September and Christmas.

CONFIDENTIALITY AND PRIVACY

It is a good idea to add a paragraph about confidentiality and privacy in the recap. As you can imagine, both of these are tantamount. The prospect has trusted you with insider knowledge that must remain private, and the terms of any deal you offer and reach must be confidential as well.

Once the sponsorship is public, of course, the dollar values or range of investment may also be made public. But the value and nature of assets purchased remains confidential, and so must what you learn about the prospect, such as the details in the Big Business Retail Conglomerate example provided.

The sponsorship world is a small community. If you release confidential information, it will come back to haunt you. You will sour the relationship with that particular sponsor, and you will make yourself unwelcome in many other companies.

ABOUT YOU

Listen carefully. For those of you who sell sponsorships, it is not about you. Sorry, let me put it a different way. For those of you who sell sponsorships, it is not about you.
- Partnership Group – Sponsorship Specialists™ blog, March 13, 2012

This section should not take long to prepare, since it should be the shortest one in the entire document. And take note, for most of you reading this book, this section will be a major paradigm shift.

Most of us are used to building a proposal that focuses 90% on us, our organization and our needs. We think it imperative to tell the prospect all about us; how many kids we helped, how many people we kept off the street, how much research we funded or that our building was blessed by the Queen! Understand that this section is a brief recap about you and the applicable elements of your organization. If your prospect doesn't know who you are or what you are about at this point, then you have not done your job so far.

Keep it to one page, and leave plenty of white space on that page. Match it exactly to the sponsorship offer. If the opportunity is to name an event, the page is about the event. If the offer is to sponsor both a golf tournament and an education program, the same page deals with the golf tournament and the education program. If the offer is to sponsor the entire organization, then the page discusses the entire organization.

Tie it logically to the proposal as a whole, which is focused on what the prospect needs and what specific benefits the property can offer to meet those needs. You can do that by referring to how you have customized the program for the prospect by choosing the particular assets and benefits that best suit its goals.

Do not include anything in this section that is essential to the prospect's understanding of the partnership you are offering. It may not be read, or if read, may not be remembered because good sponsorship officers focus first and foremost on their employer's business objectives.

This sample page from World Vision Canada is used with the organization's permission. It demonstrates how a full range of programs and achievements can be condensed to a one-page description.

WORLD VISION CANADA – AN INTRODUCTION:

World Vision is a Christian humanitarian organization serving the world's poor and displaced. This assistance is offered without regard to people's religious beliefs, gender or ethnic background. World Vision is Canada's largest international aid organization, with over 500,000 donors supporting 249 projects and 497,000 sponsored children in 49 countries. We work in partnership with individuals, corporations and governments to provide programs that help save lives, bring hope and restore dignity.

5 Unique World Vision Canada Properties:

> **30-Hour Famine** – The 30-Hour Famine acts as World Vision's primary channel for reaching Canadian youth through PR, media exposure and word of mouth. The Famine began in Calgary 33 years ago, and has grown to become a global event, with over 21 countries holding similar events. Since its inception Famine has had more than 650,000 participants who combined to donate close to $75 million. The target audience is 12-19 years of age, in secondary school.

> **Gift Catalogue** – The World Vision Christmas Gift Catalogue Campaign is a major program that brings Christmas to life by giving hope to those in need. Canadians can help transform lives by donating to categories ranging from livestock, education, micro-enterprise, agricultural, nutrition, water and much more. The program raises approximately $10M annually. Each year more than 200,000 World Vision Gifts are purchased by Canadians to help children and families in more than 39 countries. Not only has it touched lives internationally, Canadians at home can also experience the joy of fund-raising through group activities in schools, churches and workplaces.

> **The ONE LIFE Experience** is a 2,000 square-foot interactive village that will transport you to the heart of Africa. Through a captivating audio tour and powerful imagery, you will experience the impact of HIV and AIDS by stepping into the life of a child. You will gain a new and compelling understanding of the greatest humanitarian crisis of our time. World Vision's ONE LIFE Experience Canadian Tour was launched in August 2007 at West Edmonton Mall and has since made stops in

Winnipeg, Kelowna, Calgary, Regina, Montreal, Kitchener, Toronto, St. Catharines, Langley, Victoria, Burnaby, Saskatoon and Grande Prairie. The ONE LIFE Experience is currently housed at West Edmonton Mall, where it continues to educate the public and compel them to take action through child sponsorship

> **Childview Magazine** – Childview has been World Vision's magazine for Canadian child sponsors since 1987. This full colour, 24-page twice-yearly publication is available in both English and French. The magazine informs readers about World Vision's work, motivates them to act and shows them how their donations are making a difference.

> **Youth Leadership ACTIVATE Event** A day you don't want to miss! In one day, 30-Hour Famine student leaders discover the underlying causes of poverty, the stark inequalities of the world we live in and how they can contribute to lasting change through:

> > Dynamic keynote speakers talking about issues of food security and hunger
> > Impactful interactive global simulation game
> > Multimedia presentations
> > Peer-to-peer learning and workshops
> > Small group discussions
> > Come to understand the real issues and get inspired to do something real.

8
WHAT TO INCLUDE: OFFER OF BENEFITS

If you are a property, what differentiates you from other properties? Sure, you are a food bank and they are a hospice, or you are hockey and they are a municipal recreation centre. Truly, you are different then. To the sponsor, though, you are not different. The hospices, the youth sports team, the recreation centre and the food banks are the same. In fact, you are the same as the local paper, the pro sports team, and the radio station. The savvy sponsors will use the one (or more) of you that can best reach their audience and deliver results in the most cost-efficient manner. If you can do that for $20,000 and the newspaper or sport organization can too, why should the sponsor buy you over them?
– Partnership Group – Sponsorship Specialists™ blog, November 22, 2011)

In this section you will include the complete list of benefits and assets you propose for this particular prospect. Make sure that every benefit on that list is actually beneficial to the prospect. If they tell you they don't need event tickets, don't include them! They do not find these of value! Define clearly how each benefit will assist the prospect to achieve their goals. Write as though the proposal will have to convince someone who hasn't been part of your earlier meetings.

"Sponsorships can go wrong when the property takes for granted that you want the usual table, the usual signage. I want something more creative. Do your homework. You should know coming in to see me that I'm reaching out to kids over 18. 'You're big in the community. You should be there' – that means nothing."
*– **Toni Ennis**, the manager of marketing, advertising and events for a national Canadian insurance company*

If the prospect has asked you to build more than one benefit package at different price levels, start with the highest value one – it will be the most exciting for the decision maker, and placing it first will give you a greater chance of acceptance. For every benefit, describe its potential impact on the sponsor's business goals.

EXAMPLE:
ABC Supermarkets will receive 20 banners, even though the normal benefit is 10 at this investment level. During our discussions, you clearly identified branding as a goal. In response to that, we would like to

offer you additional banners. We will locate these at entrances and exits so that festival customers will see your branding material at least three times: when they enter, when they pass by the food vendors, and when they leave.

> Because ABC Supermarkets indicated a desire for one-on-one time offsite with its franchisees, we would like to offer you not only the tickets, which will allow you to meet franchisees individually, but a private hospitality suite to support high-quality conversations.

If your mission and impact relates in some way to the prospect's goals, point that out during the benefits offer.

> Like ABC Supermarkets, the Fabulicious Festival reaches an audience that values fresh, nutritious food. Patron surveys have shown that 88% of those attending are looking for information about where to buy ingredients for healthy meals."

As well as demonstrating how each benefit meets an objective for the sponsor and how it fits with the property's audience, give specifications for anything the sponsor must provide, pay for or do. With banners, for example, indicate the number, required size, shape, quality, hanging style, delivery date and location.

A complex sponsorship may have a large number of benefits. Numbering them and listing no more than three on a page will give each one the spotlight it deserves and make it easier to find for future discussion.

To make your list even more manageable, arrange the benefits in groups such as hospitality, recognition outside the event, employee engagement opportunities, media exposure, signage, tickets, and unique benefits not offered to other sponsors. Put one of your most exciting assets at the beginning of the list, and one right at the end, just before the total rights fee. This ensures there is a "hot button" item at the beginning to get them excited as well as at the end to make sure they stay excited.

A note about contra or Value In Kind (VIK) arrangements: Be very sure that you and the prospect are delivering equal value. For example, you should agree on whether to use wholesale or retail values when describing the worth of what is provided from each of you. With a media package, use what clients would actually pay, not what the rate sheet says or the inflated media numbers.

EXAMPLE:

Refer again to the Canadian Tire/ Livegreen Toronto sponsorship described in the Discovery section. In the proposal to Canadian Tire, the City clearly laid out how the money that Canadian Tire had allocated for its direct mail campaign would be more effectively spent on reaching a selected target market through the City's water bill mailings. In your proposals, be sure to look for opportunities to show a sponsor how your benefits will deliver better results for the amount of money they are now spending on TV, radio, out-of-home channels or newspaper advertising.

It is also critical to understand that you do not accept a contra/VIK deal unless you can offset that amount for a budgeted line item.

So when a car dealer says, "I don't actually have the $40,000 in cash to do this deal, but I will give you a truck for the $40,000 value," your answer is emphatically "no" unless your organization has already budgeted or is willing to budget $40,000 for a new truck.

Or, when the chocolate bar company tells you it will supply 2000 fancy chocolate bars worth $2 for each participants' registration kit, it may claim that those bars are worth a $4,000 sponsorship. Again, unless you budgeted for a chocolate bar for each person in their kits, this is not a deal for you!

Your answer is "Great! You can buy a $2,500 sponsorship for cash, which will give you the right to include your chocolate bars in delegate kits!" You get $2500 cash, and they get a banner, a logo inclusion, the right to sample their product, and whatever else you both agree would fit into the customized $2500 package.

> **EXERCISE**
> *Think about the property you have analyzed in earlier exercises – one with which you are familiar through attendance, volunteer participation or employment. List three benefits it could offer to a sponsor, suggest the right sponsor, and describe in detail how each benefit would help to meet that sponsor's business objectives. Explain how one of the benefits would be more effective than something the company already does or is planning to do. Create an imaginary scenario here if you do not have the details you need.*

ALWAYS BUNDLE YOUR BENEFITS

When your cable company offers you a "bundle" of benefits, it has completely missed the point. Bundling does not mean creating two or three levels of benefits (or channels) and offering the same bundles to all customers. Bundling does not mean forcing customers to take channels they never watch and depriving them of some they want unless they take even more they do not want.

If your cable company truly understood bundling, it would ask you which channels you wanted and build you a bundle of services based on everything you want to watch and nothing you do not want. That is what you need to do with your property's assets and benefits to create a truly successful sponsorship. You put together the right benefits to meet the business needs of that particular prospect.

Done strategically, bundling will create more revenue for you and deliver better results for your sponsor. Bundling is one of the core features of customized proposals. A series of assets that the sponsor needs to achieve business goals is bundled together in one package, a package that would be unique to that sponsor, just like the Coke/Pepsi scenario referred to in the previous chapter.

Be cautious with sponsors that appear to be focused on spending as little as possible. That approach is often a sign that they don't really understand what you have available or what they need. Use your discovery time wisely to help them pinpoint what they need, and reflect that back in a bundle of benefits that addresses each need.

> **EXERCISE**
> *What do you imagine are the business objectives for The Bay? Select a sponsorship property, perhaps the one you have used in other exercises. What benefits would you bundle for The Bay and what benefits would you not offer?*
>
> *Now go through the same exercise for an accounting firm such as Deloitte and an investment broker such as Scotia Capital Markets. What benefits would you bundle for them, and what benefits would you not offer?*

It is never wise to sell your benefits "à la carte" or one at a time. Sponsors often do not see tangible results from such limited involvement, and it puts you in the position of selling a product rather than a partnership. Benefits often strengthen each other when they are bundled together. Demonstrating that to your prospect will actually increase their value and bring you more revenue.

9
WHAT TO INCLUDE: INVESTMENT AND DISCOUNT; LEGAL AND CLOSING

INVESTMENT AND DISCOUNT

To be taken seriously as a sponsorship seller, you must use real market value for the benefits you offer. As indicated in Chapter 2, use industry standard values and if possible, hire a professional for that portion of your sponsorship strategy at least. Remember:

> > It doesn't matter what you think the benefit is worth.
> > It doesn't matter what other properties get.
> > It doesn't matter what you need to cover your costs.
> > It doesn't matter what the prospect has to spend.

All that matters is the right list of benefits at the right values.

It is no different than the manufacturer's suggested retail price (MSRP) for a car, or the line rate for a newspaper buy, or the price on the shelf with the cans of soup. Everything has a market value, and you need to know what that value is for every single asset you propose in a pitch. Your transparency and integrity will set you apart from your competition. Others will ask for what they need or think they can get. You, by contrast, will be professional, which will go a long way for a long time! Using the inventory values discussed in Chapter 2, show the total precise value of the bundled list of benefits. The actual investment from the sponsor should be a round number approximating 85% of the true market value – "This package is worth $25,256.97. Your investment is $23,200 + GST."

Experienced sponsorship buyers expect a greater discount for a higher level of sponsorship. For a $1.5 million annual sponsorship investment you may be able to offer a 33% discount to $1 million if there are no major hard costs. At the other end of the scale, for a package with the value of $1,000, you may want to only offer a 10% discount, or a price of $900.

Emphasize that you are reporting true value based on industry standards, not an inflated, unfounded number, and that you have not included superfluous, unnecessary benefits that are irrelevant to the prospect's business objectives. This is the essence of custom-designed proposals. This is what sponsors are looking for.

This is what garners the most revenue for your property and the best ROI for your sponsor.

Why would you sell a sponsorship for less than 100% of value? Frankly, it is a recommended negotiating tactic because nobody expects to pay the manufacturer's suggested price. Discounting up front signals that you have just made your best offer and also illustrates that you are offering a great deal.

And remember, that it is a genuine discount from real market value, not from a value that has been artificially inflated so that you can pretend to discount it more. That pretense is crazy, but often practiced by those who fail in the long run. Such sellers might claim, for instance, that their value is $25,000 (a figure too often picked out of the air) but they will sell it for $5,000 and provide a 5:1 "value." In reality, any experienced buyer will recognize that the package isn't worth $25,000. Those sellers end up looking like stereotypical used car salesmen.

There is a difference in quality and performance between a Focus and a Lincoln. If I want a luxury car with comfort and all the bells and whistles, I will pay the extra money for the Lincoln. As a property, your products are different from others and you need to show why, along with how you can deliver results accordingly, to overcome a price objection.
– Partnership Group – Sponsorship Specialists™ blog, February 7, 2012

If the prospect wants a lower price after you have discounted from the genuine market value, there is only one way to create it: offer a smaller program. Industry standard values prove that the market value for your initial offer is correct. You have already demonstrated good faith and a hunger for the deal by offering an initial discount. The prospect's only choice now is to pay your price or accept a smaller program.

(You may, however, choose to offer an option which still respects the value of your benefit package: if the prospect commits to a multi-year program, you could offer either a further discount or a guarantee that the price will not increase in subsequent years.)

The investment and discount section is also the place to address the sponsor's return on investment (ROI). While ROI is extremely important to sponsors, they don't necessarily allocate the funds to achieve and measure it. Sponsors don't need to be

Dow Chemical or Coca-Cola to measure their ROI. They just need a plan and a goal. No matter the investment level, if they have a goal, it can be measured. Whether the sponsorship investment is to increase government contracts like Dow, or get pouring rights and case lot sales like Coke, measurement of original goals is critical. But sometimes those goals are not so tangible. Perhaps the sponsor invests to achieve employee engagement, retention or acquisition, a product launch or brand awareness. It doesn't matter. As long as sponsors know what they want to achieve and can set goals, they can measure ROI.

Encourage your sponsors to set goals and objectives to measure their success at the end of the project – perhaps a 25% increase in sales, or an 8% increase in unaided brand recall, or a 13% increase in employee satisfaction. Note that for the latter two examples a sponsor will require additional investment to determine the pre-sponsorship brand recall or employee satisfaction level and then a post-sponsorship analysis as well.

What if your assets aren't worth much? If your awareness of industry standard values suggests that your values will be very low, do not go through the exercise of valuing them in the first place. Once you know what they are worth, you are morally bound to disclose the values in sponsorship proposals. No, you will not be able to demonstrate dollar value, and yes, an experienced prospect will notice that those numbers are missing. But, if you can demonstrate how everything you propose to do will meet a prospect's objectives, you still have a right to submit once you are asked, and you still stand a chance of securing the agreement.

EXAMPLE:

The Airdrie Festival of Lights, a Christmas lighting festival in a bedroom community near Calgary, Alberta, used that strategy successfully. They enriched their benefit package with additional useful assets such as a hosting tent, rides, activities and new signage as well as highlighting their most exciting achievement: their rapidly growing audience. With that information, they were able to move 31 sponsors, one for each night of the festival, from $500 to $1000. They doubled their money in three days of renewal activity even though they did not conduct a valuation. But they did follow their consultant's direction on taking a different approach that would generate additional revenue for the festival and better ROI for the sponsors.

LEGAL AND CLOSING

Include a signing page in the proposal rather than as a separate document. The proposal itself should be the clearest possible description of the partnership so that you will not need a lawyer to prepare a multi-page contract reiterating its terms. You should, however, seek legal help on the signing page. Your lawyers should also review the entire document template to make sure you are not at risk.

The signature page should include a clear description of the value and the investment, the terms of payment, and the payment due dates or instalment timetable.

The following example, provides a template for your signature page.

SIGNATURE PAGE (TEMPLATE)

As the (Title, Presenting, other) Sponsor of ABC Organization you will receive the following elements:

1.   Your logo will be included on our sponsor page in the program, which will illustrate your commitment to our organization and assist in building your brand and image in our community.

2.   You will have the opportunity at three events per year to provide samples of your product to our patrons as they exit the event (product and labour for sampling to be provided by the sponsor above and beyond the investment in this agreement).

3.   You will have the opportunity for…. (List all benefits)

Should any location not be available due to circumstances beyond the control of ABC Organization, reasonable replacement value will be delivered by ABC Organization.

This opportunity is offered for a minimum 3-year term.

Annual Program Value: $12,345.83
ANNUAL INVESTMENT: $10,000.00 plus applicable taxes

A Tax Receipt will not be issued, as this is considered a marketing investment and not a donation.

All amounts to be paid in accordance with the sponsorship agreement shall be paid without deduction of any taxes, levies, duties, charges or expenses whatsoever. Specifically it is agreed that as well as the consideration provided hereunder, the Sponsor shall also pay thereon applicable sales taxes, or such other sales tax or value-added tax that may be imposed.
ADDITIONAL ELEMENTS:

This agreement may be terminated for any one or more of the following events:

(i)   if a party fails to make payments when due hereunder and such remain unpaid after ten (10) days' notice thereof; or

(ii)   if a party shall have a receiver, manager, receiver-manager or trustee appointed with respect to all or substantially all of its assets or undertakings and such appointment remains undischarged for thirty (30) days; or

(iii)   if any order is made or a resolution is passed for the winding-up of a party and such continues undismissed for thirty (30) days; or

(iv)   if a party has all or substantially all of its assets taken in enforcement or collection proceedings and such appointment remains undischarged for thirty (30) days; or

(v)   if a party makes an assignment or is petitioned into bankruptcy and such remains undismissed for a period of thirty (30) days; or

(vi)   if a party breaches this Agreement and such defaulting party fails to cure such breach within thirty (30) days of receipt of written notice of such breach, then the party who is not the defaulting party may terminate this Agreement without notice to the defaulting party; or

(vii)   in the event that the other party fails to perform any of its material obligations hereunder and such failure is not remedied as soon as possible, but no later than thirty (30) days following notice.

The parties acknowledge that this Agreement does not constitute an association for the purpose of establishing a partnership or joint venture and does not create an agency relationship between the parties.

_____   _____
Accepted for (insert name of prospect)   Date

_____   _____
Your Organization Name Here   Date

OTHER ELEMENTS OF THE PROPOSAL

Before submitting your proposal, confirm your prospect's preference for hard or soft copy and Word, PDF or PowerPoint format. You may be able to add other elements to the proposal or the presentation meeting: inviting the prospect to your location if it's glamorous or mysterious, presenting the document in a gift or product box, using mock signage, or playing a video message from a celebrity whose participation is confirmed. You might also discuss additional activation ideas and their likely costs.

Rehearse your presentation carefully. Do a dry run in front of two or three people whose feedback you trust. Think about a personality or local celebrity you might take with you to the presentation meeting – a star player, a leading dancer, your artistic director – and prepare that person thoroughly. But do not be distressed if some of your presentation plans fall through. What ultimately sells the proposal is not the flash and glamour, but the business benefits – the content of your document. Stay grounded in that, know your content cold, and your presentation will do justice to your proposal.

When making the final presentation, start by reiterating that it's based on information you've discovered over the past months, and ask if anything has changed. If there's been a big change that invalidates some of your components, go back into discovery mode right there. Ask for the chance to learn more and revise your proposal.

WHAT ABOUT ONLINE SPONSORSHIP APPLICATIONS?

It is becoming harder and harder to build relationships with businesses. More and more players enter the sponsorship-selling field each year. Both sponsors and prospects experience more turnover, which means that relationships have to be rebuilt. More unsolicited and unprofessional submissions are being sent to sponsors, and as recognition of sponsorship's huge potential grows, the industry is becoming more competitive.

To cut the clutter and be able to stay focused on objectives, many brands and sponsors have gone to online submissions. These online systems are fantastic for sponsors and can be efficient for sellers as well. In most cases, there is no way around the requirement. If you must submit online, you have no choice. But even with an online application, you can set yourself apart by building a face-to-face relationship first.

A prospect's request for an online application does not rule out a chance to build a good relationship before submitting. Go through the discovery in person or by telephone. Get your proposal evaluated first, just as you would without the online process. If you develop a good relationship you can have your champion review the proposal, make suggested changes, and for the most part, endorse it even before you take it to the online submission.

When you finally use the online process, you will be able to submit a proposal that the prospect has already vetted. By then, the prospect's sponsorship manager is only waiting for the online proposal as the last formality to close the deal.

There is no substitute for personal relationships. Even when proposals must be submitted online, sponsorship managers are always willing to see someone who is more interested in their company's objectives than in selling.

> **EXERCISE**
> *Using the property and the business prospect from your earlier exercises, prepare a complete proposal from the property to the prospect. If you are not fully knowledgeable about the two parties, go ahead and invent what the property can offer and what the company's objectives are.*

TO SUM UP

Here are ten tips that will make your proposal a successful sales document.

1. Know what you have to sell.

2. Know the value of your assets.

3. Go through a thorough discovery process.

4. Customize the proposal.

5. Do not sell or pitch a stock package.

6. Make the proposal about the sponsor, not about your organization.

7. Ensure the benefits you offer will assist the sponsor to meet their goals, not yours.

8. Show the value in dollars and the investment in dollars.

9. Ensure the proposal is detailed and covers all parties legally.

10. Deliver the proposal in the format the sponsor needs or wants.

In Sample Three, pages 157-172 we have provided a full proposal for your reference.

Sponsorship is a business transaction. If your prospects cared only about your mission and outcomes and were not looking for any business benefit or ROI, they'd give you money and expect nothing in return. That is called philanthropy and there is very little of that in today's business world.
– Partnership Group – Sponsorship Specialists™ workshop, Ottawa, June 2013

ACTIVATION – GETTING SPONSORS TO ACTIVATE

REALITY
CHECK

REALITY CHECK – WHEN ACTIVATION FAILS, THE SPONSORSHIP FAILS.

"I've seen sponsorships go wrong through a lack of activation. Perhaps the corporate decision-maker changes, and there's no follow through when the file is passed on. Sometimes there's no marketing department involvement, or no business objective behind the sponsorship." – Suzanne Mott, Vertigo Theatre, Calgary

In this section, you will read about dozens of successful, creative activation ideas that will inspire you to look for similar opportunities within your own property. You will learn how to include them in the agreement and ensure that there is a budget for their delivery, even when the sponsor pays for them. And you will learn how to track the success of each activation tactic and report it back to the sponsor.

10
WHY ACTIVATION MATTERS

In Canada, the steps of research, discovery, proposal writing and negotiation typically continue for 18 to 22 months. During that time, it is all too easy for both property and prospect to concentrate on a good match between benefits and business objectives, the innumerable details of signage and media coverage, and the costs of sponsorship. Do not let all of that distract you or your prospect from the most crucial element of all – activation. The real work begins after the deal is signed!

WHEN ACTIVATION FAILS, THE SPONSORSHIP FAILS

Activation makes the difference between a sponsorship that is unremarkable and one that is a knockout success. Marketing-savvy sponsors will enthusiastically propose a raft of activation ideas that fulfil business objectives and help to deliver ROI. But others, particularly those who confuse sponsorship with philanthropy, may think their job is done once the contract is signed.

In that case, the property must emphasize the importance of activation, help the sponsor develop tactics, incorporate those tactics into the sponsorship agreement, and hold the sponsor accountable for implementing their part of the activation plan.

> **EXAMPLE:**
> An engineering firm was the title sponsor for a golf tournament held by a youth services nonprofit in Edmonton. Among the activation tactics in the agreement were:
> > The right to provide branded clothing for tournament volunteers;
> > The chance to speak during the dinner that concluded the tournament;
> > The right to hang eight banners in the banquet room;
> > The opportunity to place a premium for each guest on the dinner tables; and
> > The chance to have a staff member at every table.

When the engineering firm announced that it did not intend to take advantage of the benefits related to the banquet – in essence, withdrawing from much of its activation – the youth organization warned them that the sponsorship would be less effective as a result.

By contrast, the credit union that had paid a smaller sponsorship fee to be the presenting sponsor of the dinner deployed the full range of activation techniques in its agreement. It outshone the engineering firm to the point that some guests thought the credit union, not the engineering firm, was the primary tournament sponsor.

The engineering firm met with the youth organization, indignant and ready to criticize them for mishandling the evening and favouring the credit union. Fortunately, the youth organization was able to pull out the agreement and point to all the contractual activation techniques the engineering company had not carried out.

When a sponsor falls short on its part of the activation agreement, it will inevitably be disappointed in the sponsorship. In the preceding example, the sponsor at first blamed the property. A valuable, high-potential business relationship could have been lost.

In such a case, the property's best approach is to say, "I can help you get better results than that. You did have these things you could have done, rights you had already paid for. When we do this again, you may have to spend a little more to achieve your goal, but it will be worth it. You and I put a lot of thought into your activation strategy, and I still believe it is right for you. I will work with you next time to make these tactics effective. Then if you still do not get the results you want, we can change our contract and find other ways to achieve your goals."

The next year the engineering firm returned. And they activated. They received kudos from participants and their clients for their "support" of the charity as well compliments from employees who felt proud to be associated with the event. The goals had been to build employee engagement (which soared when many volunteered to work at the tournament) and profile in the community. The activation paid off!

It's like buying a car. You pay for the car and all the gadgets, but if you do not spend some extra money to buy gas, oil, new tires when necessary, and regular tune-ups, the car won't work. It's the money you spend after you buy the car that makes it work.

Sponsors need to remember this. They must pay for the rights fee, but then they must also invest in outside elements afterward, such as marketing the relationship, hosting and hospitality, employee engagement and so on. Great car dealers offer such "activation," often with a preferred rate for tune-ups and lifelong oil changes, to ensure that the customer comes back. (Let's face it, though. You are paying for all of that somewhere!) If sponsors do not activate, they do not see results and their sponsorship will, like the car, eventually stop working. When that happens, the property doesn't get the money!

Sponsors, remember you need to add gas to your investment. Properties, remember you need to make sure the sponsors add gas… leave them money to do so! If both these things happen, the partnership will continue for a long time!
– Partnership Group – Sponsorship Specialists™ blog September 13, 2011

Lack of activation was one of the principal disappointments identified in the *2012 Canadian Sponsorship Landscape Study*. If a company does not spend on activation, the money paid for its sponsorship rights fee is wasted. When a sponsorship buyer does not realize that activation is essential, the property must take the lead in two ways:

1. Include activation as a topic in the discovery sessions, the proposal and the sponsorship contract. When the deal is signed, the sponsor is obligated to carry out certain activation tactics. A total plan is the better approach for the long term.

2. Probe the sponsor's business needs to discover activation tactics that will make the sponsorship successful. Properties must encourage sponsors to spend more money on activation – not necessarily with them, but wherever it will make the most impact on the sponsorship investment.

Sponsorship cannot happen successfully in a silo. It is an integrated marketing medium. Too often, brands buy sponsorship and think that it will create reach and brand awareness, drive traffic and engage employees. Yes, it can do all that and more. But it needs help from several company departments: media, investor relations, public relations, government relations, human resources and so on.

For example, when sponsors name employee engagement as one of their objectives, encourage them to embrace the sponsorship in the employee newsletter, run "lunch and learn" events, undertake educational opportunities, and feature sponsorship news on their Facebook pages, as well as intranet and internal employee communications. Unless the sponsor communicates with its staff, they cannot engage and embrace.

The same goes for external objectives. If the goal is to drive store traffic, there must be a media or social media campaign. The sponsor must let its customers and the property's constituents know of its affinity with the property and drive traffic accordingly. In a retail campaign, the sponsor must also communicate to the people on the front line at the retail stores.

When we launched a campaign for Harvey's restaurants with the Calgary Flames Hockey Club and its mascot "Harvey the Hound," it was done at the Saddledome with all the store staff on site. The staff learned about the promotion, the sponsorship, the traffic they would see, and how the program worked. The staff got a building tour, met Harvey and the Flame players and went home with gifts. That campaign delivered double-digit lift to the restaurant chain in Calgary, while the national growth that year was less than one percent. The campaign was supported by commercials on radio as well as live on-site radio remotes with Harvey the Hound. It is critical to communicate your sponsorship, or it is dead before you pay the first installment on the rights fee!
– Partnership Group – Sponsorship Specialists™ blog June 25, 2013

In 2012, sponsors spent an additional $0.75 on activation for every dollar they spent on sponsorship rights fees *(2013 Canadian Sponsorship Landscape Study)*. While a hard and fast ratio is not helpful, many successful sponsors find that the right spend is closer to $3 for every dollar on rights fees.

For the 2010 Olympics, Bell Canada invested about $80 million to be a sponsor. That bought them the right to use the Olympic rings in their materials and to be the event's official telecommunications company. Nothing else was included – no tickets, no signage, no other benefits.

Then Bell invested about $320 million on media buys, mitten giveaways, tickets, client hospitality and athlete sponsorships. Not all of it was new money. Some of the advertising, for instance, would have been done anyway through other channels. Spending four times the rights fee on activation made the sponsorship memorable for consumers and successful for Bell. Bell measured this success by *retail sales increases, brand recall and market share increase. All were positive and exceeded expectations. It was a great investment for Bell, and it was activation that made it work. (Partnership Group – Sponsorship Specialists™ activation workshop, Ottawa, June 2013)*

When sponsors are not willing to spend on activation, it can be more palatable to build the costs of some activation tactics (gala tickets or hotel rooms arranged by the property) into the rights fee itself, provided that both parties agree that the tactics help the sponsor to meet its objectives. Charities, which as a sector have captured a higher share of the sponsorship market than sports properties, often follow that strategy. Sports properties and others may have to educate the sponsors about why activation costs are included in the agreement.

As a property, your job is to create success for your sponsors. Are they interested in boosting sales? Store traffic? Brand awareness? Staff engagement? Ask specific questions about their priorities. Once you know your sponsors' goals, come to them with activation ideas that meet their needs and budget.

WHEN TO WALK AWAY

If your sponsors are not sophisticated enough to understand activation, they may not let you build activation tactics into the agreement. At some point you will have to decide whether the sponsorship can be truly successful if the sponsors will not activate. It is always your responsibility to point out the need for activation. The time may come when you will have to end negotiations and move on to a partner with whom you can craft a more effective sponsorship.

At times, corporations increase their sponsorship activities because they need positive media attention. When BHP Billiton launched its 2010 takeover attempt of Saskatchewan's Potash Corporation, both companies made significant new sponsorship investments in Saskatoon, announcing them just one day apart. Saskatchewan Potash continues to be dominant in the market space because of its ongoing valuation and activation tactics to ensure they are receiving measurable ROI.

A few months after the disastrous Deepwater Horizon oil spill off coastal Louisiana, British Petroleum enhanced its partnership with the 2012 Olympics in London to redeem its image. If you accept a sponsorship where such needs apply, be sure you can stand up in front of your own constituents and the media while stating with integrity that you are "proud to partner" with the image-afflicted sponsor. If you cannot, then do not accept or solicit the sponsorship.

Another instance in which you and your sponsor may not agree is the issue of control. Sponsors pay a rights fee to be associated with your brand and meet your audience, not to run your property. Sponsorship does not imply the right to control hiring, vet the choice of a theatre's plays or personnel, control or restrict academic research and teaching, or dictate event logistics. When such expectations surface and cannot be negotiated away, it is best to thank the prospect for their time and bow out.

11
EXAMPLES OF ACTIVATION TACTICS

In an earlier section, you learned that the list of a property's benefits is almost always far larger than you might think. The same is true for activation tactics. The two are related because every opportunity to activate is also a benefit, and they are limited only by the creativity of the property and the sponsor. An unrelenting focus on the sponsor's business objectives will help both sponsor and property to focus on the most effective benefits from the initial list.

PUBLIC RELATIONS LEVERAGING

Does your sponsor need support in the area of public relations, either because they are building up their profile and brand or because their image has taken a beating? Will an additional investment outside your property help them to reach their goal? If so, then both sponsor and property should work together to leverage the opportunities that each one can offer.

A great example of a sponsorship leveraging a PR campaign was British Petroleum (BP)'s involvement with the 2012 London Olympics. As discussed earlier, it was already a top tier sponsor. When the Deepwater Horizon oil spill occurred, BP enhanced its investment. The London Olympics CEO stood on a podium with the BP CEO to thank BP, promote BP as a great partner, and assure the public that BP cared about the environment and would clean up the Gulf of Mexico mess. That was important positioning for BP.

Today, BP is a major sponsor of the Florida and Louisiana tourism bureaus. It invests millions in direct sponsorship as well as activation programs to provide discounted gas coupons for visitors. This again helps rebuild its public image in areas that were so detrimentally affected by the oil spill.

SAMPLING

Events offer a great opportunity to place new products into the hands of participants who match the sponsor's target market. As mentioned in Chapter 3, the value of a sampling opportunity increases with the degree of fit between the property's audience and the sponsor's market, and with the opportunity to present the product personally. Thorough activation can make the difference that turns sampling into sales.

Sampling also offers a sponsor one of the best ways to test or launch a new product. When Listerine sampled its antiseptic throat lozenges at the Edmonton Fringe Festival, the company also had a budget to ship the samples, hire onsite staff to distribute the product and place point-of-purchase material in convenience stores. At every festival venue where Listerine sampled, nearby convenience stores sold out of the product within 24 hours. If Listerine had just bought the rights and not activated, they would not have achieved that level of success.

Highly creative sampling may even involve giving away something other than the sponsor's product. For example, geoLOGIC Systems is an Alberta-based international software company focused on data, mapping and analysis tools for the petroleum industry. They had always given away flash drives loaded with software samples in the delegate bags at a conference where they were one of the sponsors.

The tactic, though typical for a software developer, was not personal. In previous years, the flash drives were buried amongst the other materials in the bags. There was no incentive for delegates to visit geoLOGIC's booth and learn more about the project. To meet the objective of generating sales leads and personal demonstration opportunities at the booth, the company and the conference brainstormed with the Partnership Group – Sponsorship Specialists™ to build a better activation and sponsorship program.

At a plenary luncheons that geoLOGIC sponsored, the ice cream dessert was not served at the tables. Instead, delegates had to pick it up at geoLOGIC's booth. The company sweetened the offer by pledging a $1 charitable donation for every scoop it served.

geoLOGIC's closing ratio of getting face-to-face meetings with prospects in their offices after the conference jumped from 20% in previous conferences to 68%. The sample was ice cream – a much more appealing item than a flash drive – and the sales pitch happened while people stood in line.

The tactic involved extra activation expenses for geoLOGIC. They had to double the size of their booth and have far more staff on hand for the ice cream giveaway. They also incurred the expense of the charitable donation. But their closing ratio more than tripled and they built the extra goodwill of publicly supporting a charity on behalf of the delegates.

ACTIVATION

A little more money on activation, a much greater measurable result!

HOSTING OR HOSPITALITY

Even after agreeing that hosting or hospitality opportunities fit with their business objectives, too many companies fail to budget for them. Properties may have to help sponsors understand what they are getting, how they will use it, and what extra commitments they need to make to shine while sponsoring.

For example, if a property contributes the benefit of a table at a gala, the sponsor becomes a host and must think about the full range of hospitality normally offered to guests. That may mean budgeting for things like drinks and overnight accommodation or limo transport to and from the event. The sponsor's guests should not have to reach into their own pockets for anything that feels like an integral part of the evening. Alert your sponsor to consider buying raffle tickets, silent auction items, balloon prizes, and anything else that seems like an important part of the event.

DRIVING SALES

Even without sampling, activation can turn a sponsorship into a sales tool with measurable results. Consider the example of Molson Old Style Pilsner's status as the official brewery of the Saskatchewan Roughriders. Increasing market share in liquor stores was one objective of the sponsorship – but sampling was not a permissible tactic.

In 2007 Molson launched a meaningful giveaway tied to its sponsorship. It added car window flags for the Roughriders to specially branded cases of 24 bottles of Pilsner. Molson also negotiated front-of-aisle store positioning for the branded cases and promoted them heavily. By any measure, the tactic was a huge success. Months after the initial spike, sales of the 24-bottle cases of Pilsner stayed about 30% higher than they had been before the promotion.

SPEAKING OPPORTUNITIES

Most sponsors perceive high value in having their president or vice-president speak to a desirable audience, especially if there will be sound bites on local media or additional interviews tied to the speech.

Consumers, though, have a different opinion. They rank sponsor speeches as one of the least influential sponsorship tactics *(2012 Consumer Sponsorship Rankings).*

Consider showing brief sponsor speeches via video rather than letting several people speak live, with the risk of running overtime and detracting from the social nature of a gala or reception. Or restrict speaking opportunities to the title sponsor. There is one effective way for sponsors to exploit a speech – keep it short and use it to introduce a celebrity associated with the event or the company. Olympic gold medalist Catriona Lemay Doan, for instance, has been a spokesperson for Saskatchewan Blue Cross since 1999. The company makes the most of any speaking opportunity that presents her and her relationship to Saskatchewan Blue Cross – and audiences love it!

COUPONS AND BOUNCE-BACK OFFERS

Coupons and other bounce-back offers are intended to drive customer traffic and increase sales. To work effectively, they must be trackable (the customer activates an event-specific code or hands over the coupon) and time-limited.

When Banana Republic Clothing Store activated on their sponsorship with the Toronto Symphony Orchestra (TSO) they offered a time limited "bounce back" coupon to those attending the concerts. Each attendee was presented with a coupon with a generous discount value valid for 14 days from the performance date. During the two-week period after each Banana Republic performance, stores saw double-digit growth in traffic and sales compared to the same period in the previous year. This is couponing at its best!

Depending on the circumstances, coupons and bounce-backs can bring sponsors and properties greater benefits than would have been gained by moving up the sponsorship ladder. From 2008-2011, Canadian Western Bank sponsored Youth Empowerment & Support Services (YESS) in Edmonton. Its principal activation tactic was selling a branded GIC (guaranteed investment certificate) and making a contribution to YESS for each one sold.

Canadian Western Bank was also the presenting sponsor of Homeless for a Night, a YESS event where participants secured donations and slept outside overnight to raise awareness of youth homelessness. The bank wanted to move up to being the event's title sponsor instead of the presenting sponsor, but had only $10,000 extra in its budget – not enough to purchase the higher-level sponsor status.

Instead, YESS urged Canadian Western Bank to spend that $10,000 difference on radio spots to promote the branded GICs more heavily. A sum that had not been enough for the title sponsorship made a real difference to GIC sales when spent with local media rather than given directly to YESS. That year, with the additional radio promotion, the GIC returned $101,000 to YESS, or $60,000 more than either of the previous two years. And the bank's revenue, of course, increased by an even greater amount.

SIGNAGE

Good signage is a basic activation tool. Be sure your contract stipulates not only the number, size and quality of the signs but the position. Any locations visible on TV coverage are premium spots and should be sold accordingly. Talk to your sponsors about whether your agreement gives them the number they would like. Be prepared to grant more if necessary, or to reduce the number if the sponsor believes it does not need them. A company primarily interested in hospitality and exclusive access to a few key clients, for instance, may not value mass recognition through signage as highly as a company that hopes to sell its product to much of your audience.

But if signage is important to your sponsors, do everything you can to encourage them to make it distinctive and creative. In most cases, better signage will boost sponsors' ROI. Exceptional signage integrates their sponsorship into their other communication programs and media campaigns.

As important as signage can be, however, it is no substitute for a full slate of activation tactics. Refer back to the example of the youth services organization and the clothing company earlier in this section for a cautionary tale on the importance of activating fully.

OTHER ACTIVATION EXAMPLES

There is no single list of activation tactics appropriate for all sponsorships – or even any sponsorship. Activation should be tailored to each partnership to make the most of opportunities that are only available in that particular combination of sponsor and property. And tactics will vary, even with the same company, between one of its sponsorships and another. The only limit on activation tactics is human creativity.

"When SaskEnergy was involved with KidSport Saskatchewan a few years ago, they wanted us to continue a sponsorship we thought had run its course. Now we also sponsored the Saskatchewan Roughriders, and felt we weren't getting the expo-

sure we needed out of that. So we set up a three-way agreement under which we provided funding for a Roughriders calendar with our name on it, and all the proceeds went to KidSport. That calendar has raised almost $1 million over five years while delivering great exposure for SaskEnergy and great publicity for the Riders."
– **Ron Podbielski**, *formerly Farm Credit Canada, SaskEnergy and SaskTel*

Here are some more activations that achieved the objectives set by sponsors. Use their ideas as a launching pad for your own imagination as you think of ways your sponsors might activate at your properties.

EXAMPLE:

McDonald's and the 2010 Vancouver Olympics
During the Olympics, McDonald's promoted its sponsorship at every one of its restaurants. When freestyle skier Alexandre Bilodeau won Canada's first Olympic gold medal on home soil, McDonald's had staff standing by on site, ready to turn that win into an activation opportunity. Within minutes, Bilodeau was at the nearest McDonald's restaurant gulping down a Big Mac and Coca-Cola in full view of the world's TV cameras.

Remax and the neighborhood block party
Strategic activation is not restricted to multi-million-dollar partnerships. At the modest end of the spectrum, a Calgary Remax agent spent $500 to sponsor a block party in a neighborhood where he hoped to gain real estate listings. Then he printed flyers to be dropped at every door in the neighborhood. He had a sign made, provided branded bottled water for the event plus logo items for children's activities, and ran an enter-to-win program to generate qualified leads. He spent more on activation than on the sponsorship fee – and he saw results. Within two years, he listed and sold two homes, both over $1 million! Not a bad ROI for his rights fee and activation investment.

12
ACTIVATION –
WHOSE JOB IS IT AND WHO PAYS?

Activation works best when both sponsor and property look out for opportunities and work together to make the most of the initiatives. Ideally, the sponsor provides cash for new media or enhancements to existing media, and brings creativity and an integrated outlook to the opportunity.

A property's flexibility and creativity go a long way towards bringing cash or value to the activation strategy. Those qualities helped the CBC create a significant activation benefit for TD Bank on the TV series **Being Erica**. TD Bank asked the CBC sponsorship sellers whether the bank could appear in episodes of the show and even whether episodes could show characters using its services.

Rather than taking that request directly to the show's executives and risking rejection of an apparent interference with content and artistic vision, the sellers started with the show's writers.

"Do you think this might work?" they asked. "Would you be able to work green and white signage into street shots? How would you build banking scenes into plot lines?"

The writers took up the creative challenge. They actually handed the sponsorship sellers some scripts for scenes that gave TD Bank the desired participation and at the same time enhanced the show. With that material in hand, the sellers had a much easier time securing management signoff on the sponsorship deal.

The property's role is first of all to be flexible and open to ideas that meet the sponsor's business goals. Properties also should bring cash or value to the deal. Remember not to grab for the last available cent. This book has already shared examples where a sponsor's spend on rights fees and strategic activation performed better for both sponsor and property than spending the entire amount on a higher-level sponsorship.

The discussion about a sponsor's responsibility to activate may have left the impression that every cost is borne by the sponsor. That may be true for such things as making banners and supplying hospitality for the sponsor's guest. But properties should not lose sight of the fact that they, too, contribute valuable assets to the activation process. Be sure to include those benefits and their value in the total investment.

Tickets to an event, for instance, have a cost to the property. They cannot be sold to anyone else if they are assigned to a sponsor. Your discovery sessions will have revealed whether the tickets are truly a benefit in the sponsor's eyes and therefore likely to be used. (Few things are more embarrassing to both parties than an extensive bank of unused seating with the sponsor's name on it.) And of course, bundling the tickets in a sponsorship package brings more revenue to your property.

But here's the catch: In most organizations, that revenue is not credited to the ticket sales budget, so you may encounter resistance and internal politics when you try to pull tickets from the box office for a sponsor. A win-win resolution might involve charging the cost of the tickets at group rates to the sponsorship budget and crediting the box office budget with the equivalent sale.

The same is true for gala tables, media ad spots, and anything else that could have been sold to patrons or used by the property if it had not been assigned to a sponsor. The property forgoes sales revenue or advertising opportunities by giving those tickets, media placements or other items to the sponsor. "Buy" them internally and then add the cost to the sponsorship package.

The services of the property's volunteers can be a significant in-kind contribution from the property. They can allow the sponsor to save on staffing costs and share the goodwill that patrons often feel towards volunteers. For example, if the sponsor trains the property's volunteers on product knowledge and supplies speaking points, volunteers can hand out the sponsor's samples.

While a sponsor must be prepared to spend on activation, not every activation tactic comes with high expenses. Business cards have to be printed anyway, so the additional expense of adding "Proud sponsor of ..." is not usually significant. That is true for properties as well – adding "Sponsored by ABC Company" to business cards and brochures that are already in the budget can boost the sponsor's ROI without a huge increase in the rights fee.

ACTIVATION

TIM HORTONS AND TIMBITS SOCCER
Children enrolled in the Timbits Soccer program bring home a huge haul of useful branded items – a sunhat, a jersey, a water bottle, a knapsack, all used at every practice and game. In a clever move to boost traffic and sales, Tim Hortons prints the words "I am thirsty" on the hemlines of the players' jerseys. Players who show their jersey hemline at a Tim Hortons counter get a free milk or juice. Often, the entire team heads for Tim's for their free beverages – bringing thirsty, hungry siblings and parents with them.

BMO AND THE TORONTO MAPLE LEAFS
At Toronto's Air Canada Centre, there are always lineups. Customers are grateful, even excited, when they are able to get in faster than they expected. While most sponsors would take their high-net-worth clients to games at the arena, BMO decided to do something for its regular customers. BMO card holders, whether they hold the World Elite charge card or the entry-level card, can go to the designated BMO door and get in without a line. BMO also gives them a free program ($12 value), a discount coupon for the building's refreshment concessions, and access to players for autographs.

WESTERNER PARK (RED DEER) AND FAS GAS
Retail gas chain Fas Gas used its sponsorship of Westerner Park in Red Deer, Alberta, to improve the performance of its flagging loyalty program economically and effectively. Fas Gas customers were logging purchases onto the company's "Litre Log" card, but weren't cashing in their earned points to get free gas. Fas Gas wanted to stimulate redemptions in order to build customer loyalty. So instead of restricting redemptions to gas, it allowed customers to spend Litre Log points on advance tickets to Westerner Days at Westerner Park.

Fas Gas spent heavily on new media to promote the opportunity. As a result, Westerner Days set a new record for advance ticket sales. Fas Gas customers started redeeming their points and continued the habit even afterwards when they could only be used on gas purchases.

All of these activation tactics worked because everyone involved was creative and the sponsors maintained an unwavering focus on their business goals and objectives. For a sponsorship to succeed, the property and the sponsor must work together, communicating frequently and openly. Both must be ready to invest time and money to make it work (although the property may be able to include some of its investment in the sponsorship rights fee). Finally, it is up to the property to deliver a rights program that can be activated above and beyond the sponsor's expectations.

TAKEAWAY TIPS

> As a property or a sponsor, make sure that activation is consistent with your brand.

> Don't worry too much about the 3:1 activation to rights fee ratio. Invest what is needed to deliver results.

> Remember, many sponsorship rights programs have activation elements already built in, so additional spending is not always required.

> Think outside the box. Do not let the words "We can't do that" or "We have never done that before" be part of your vocabulary.

> Both the sponsor and the property must invest in a successful activation program.

> Activation spends do not have to be incremental dollars – they may be accessed through existing marketing and communication budget spends.

CASE STUDY – MOXIE'S

Moxie's began as a family-oriented chain with three restaurants in Alberta. In its early days, it sponsored the Calgary Flames hockey team to attract more customers. Its primary benefit was rink boards in the Flames' home arena, the Saddledome. The sponsorship was ineffective. Why did it fail, and what might Moxie's have done with the Flames instead?

What happened: Rink boards work best in home games, where they are visible to a national television audience. The Flames had five home games that were nationally broadcast – but national visibility was wasted in the majority of communities because they lacked Moxie's restaurants. The sponsorship was deemed a failure and not renewed after its first season.

A better activation strategy for Moxie's would have been to focus on getting the Flames' home audience into its local restaurants more often. It might have bought program advertisements and space on the digital leader board to reinforce its name and brand. It might also have distributed time-limited discount coupons in the Saddledome, good for two weeks after each game, and tracked the resulting increase in traffic and sales.

The sponsorship failed because Moxie's spent its entire budget on the rights fee and accepted benefits that were ineffective for its needs. A cheaper package that included program and leader board space would have left money to absorb the impact of the lower coupon price, and would have drawn more customers to its restaurants.

Activation creates a richer experience for the property's guests or members and advances the business goals of the sponsor. A smart sponsor will look for every possible activation opportunity with its partner properties. And a smart property – your property – will emphasize activation as the key to a winning experience for everyone: the property, the sponsor and both sets of customers.

*"If the relationship is genuine and each partner is invested in the other's success, it cannot go wrong. I've never seen it in 25 years." – **Ron Podbielski**, formerly Farm Credit Canada, SaskEnergy and SaskTel*

FULFILLMENT MANAGEMENT

REALITY CHECK – IF YOU FAIL TO DELIVER ON WHAT YOU PROMISED TO DELIVER, YOUR CHANCES OF RENEWAL ARE MINIMAL.

REALITY CHECK

Closing the big deal is just the first step! Once the deal is closed, the real work begins. The focus is on fulfillment. This is critical. Whose responsibility is fulfillment? Should it be the person that sells the sponsorship? Should it be a person dedicated to fulfillment? What if you hired an outside company to sell your sponsorship assets – should they do fulfillment too?

All great questions and there is no easy answer. But whoever does the job, fulfillment is critical..

After the sponsorship has concluded – benefits delivered and activation executed – the property should deliver a fulfillment report to the sponsor within a month. That report must address every aspect of the sponsorship that was included in the contract, describing how each was achieved, even exceeded, or how and why it missed the mark.

The fulfillment report is an illustrated narrative that proves you, the property, delivered what you promised. It is an essential building block for long-term relationships and a track record of successful sponsorships. If you do it correctly, the fulfillment report and the conversation that arises out of it will serve as the first discovery tool for a renewed sponsorship between you and your sponsor-partners.

In this section, you will learn how to track fulfillment as it happens and what to include in the report.

"Our sponsors need well-done proposals, fulfillment reports, communication with our sponsorship team, and good business and human practices from us."
*– **Sue Keating**, Youth Empowerment & Support Services, Edmonton*

13
HOW TO TRACK FULFILLMENT ACTIVITIES AND REPORT TO YOUR SPONSOR

The fulfillment report is not due until the sponsorship has been fully executed. But it is dangerous to leave it until the crowds have gone home! Begin the fulfillment report immediately after you sign the contract with your sponsor.

Using your contract as your blueprint, list everything you promised to the sponsor. Determine the system you will use – spreadsheet software such as Excel, fulfillment reporting software (SAVI, for example), or even Outlook – to track what you promised to deliver. Do not assume that you will need a costly software package for this step. It is not only possible but convenient to track your fulfillment activities in a spreadsheet such as Sample 4 - the Fulfillment Spreadsheet, p.xx. Outlook is only useful for small-scale sponsorships. With task reminders and the journal, you can certainly keep tasks on track, but you will not be able to generate a report to print or email.

Whatever the means you choose, make sure that the tracking system you set up will work whether you have one sponsor or many. Tasks such as sending out tickets, bringing in banners, distributing press releases, and scheduling and holding meetings are easily forgotten unless they are all captured in your fulfillment tracking.

Stay in touch with your sponsors throughout the sponsorship. Do not assume that the fulfillment report is the only information your sponsors want! They need to hear good news and bad news, especially changes, cancellations and breaking news, before the public finds out.

If sponsors hear about the cancellation of a performer or exciting news about your organization through a third party such as a media channel, they will be annoyed. And they are right to be annoyed! Avoid that issue and make them feel appreciated by sharing insider information with them before making it public.

Make sure you write a timely fulfillment report. Submit it within one month of the sponsored event or program. With an annual contract, get the report to the sponsor before the contract period ends so you can plan together for the next contract. That might be two to three months in advance of the contract expiring.

HOW TO REPORT

Fulfillment reporting is one of the three areas that sponsors identified as most disappointing in their sponsorship experience (2012 Canadian Sponsorship Landscape Study). A comprehensive fulfillment report contains the following elements:

> A brief summary describing the event or program and the sponsor's overall investment;
> A list of what the property promised to the sponsor, taken from the contract;
> A list of how the property lived up to each promise (or did not);
> What the property did or plans to do to make up for shortfalls;
> How the property may have over-delivered on some promises;
> Pictures, video and samples of the sponsor's exposure, such as signs, their speakers, their activation, and shots of people enjoying themselves. (You will have to tell your photographer to include signage in shots, rather than considering it a distraction to avoid. Prepare a specific list of what you need photographed.

As with your proposal, present the fulfillment report by email, mailed hard copy or face to face as the sponsor chooses. Unless you know that the sponsor is impressed by elaborate formats, keep the report simple – the simpler, the better. If possible, arrange to present your fulfillment report face to face. The day before, you can also send a soft copy by email – but not early enough to allow the sponsor to say "That's all I need" and cancel the meeting.

A face-to-face presentation is important because you want to find out early about anything that didn't work for them. You also want to use the meeting as the start of discovery for the next sponsorship.

This fulfillment report can often be the basis for your contact's reporting to their superiors. A great fulfillment report will make your organization shine over the others they have invested in, and most likely will secure your renewal.

In the following pages, we are providing a fulfillment report template. It includes reporting functionality for a significant, extensive sponsorship. Yours may be simpler and shorter, but it should contain everything shown in this template.

FULFILLMENT REPORT (TEMPLATE)

<INSERT YOUR PROPERTY LOGO HERE>

**FULFILLMENT REPORT OF
<SPONSORSHIP PACKAGE DESCRIPTION>
(SUCH AS GALA BRONZE PROGAM)
FOR**

<INSERT NAME OF SPONSORING COMPANY OR ORGANIZATION>

<INSERT YOUR PROPERTY'S NAME>
ADDRESS AND WEBSITE
INSERT DATE OF REPORT DELIVERY

TABLE OF CONTENTS

Introduction   Page x

Description of sponsorship agreement   Page x

Fulfillment details   Page x

Fulfillment summary and comparables   Page x

Summary and recommendations   Page x

Appendix   Page x

INTRODUCTION

Insert the account of the specific sponsorship program the sponsor invested in – one paragraph preferably, and definitely no longer than one page.

Insert a paragraph about the sponsor and how the sponsorship was beneficial to them (as you see it).

Insert a thank-you and closing account of the impact this sponsorship had on the goal of your organization (if applicable). This should not exceed one page.

Insert a list of any media ads, print material, and logo placement for review, quotes, pictures, etc. that are included.

DESCRIPTION OF SPONSORSHIP PACKAGE

As the <insert title of sponsorship package purchased by the sponsor>, the benefits provided in your sponsorship package included:

Insert the sponsorship package that was purchased, as written in the sponsorship contract.

SPONSORSHIP PACKAGE FULFILLMENT DETAILS

In this section, provide a detailed narrative of how the sponsorship package was fulfilled or not, things that were missed, where you delivered more than promised, and how the sponsor achieved their return on investment.

This is a general, one-page report that your contact may want to pull out and submit to a superior.

Using the list of benefits in the previous section as a guide, describe:

> What was delivered as sold. (e.g., All of the signs and banners were displayed as anticipated.)

> What was over-delivered. (e.g., the two signs in foyer were prominently displayed by the entrance to the building, and due to a cancellation by another sponsor, two additional signs were provided at the doors to the theatre.)

> What was under-delivered and what you did about it. (e.g., Three of the four banners planned along the base of the stage were displayed as anticipated, however, given that the banners were longer than expected, the fourth banner was hung from the roof at centre stage, so as to be clearly visible.)

FULFILLMENT REPORT SUMMARY

Complete the table below as a point-form summary of the information provided in the two previous sections. Very briefly, list the benefits the sponsor bought and the total value of each in the left column, and the corresponding fulfillment details and values in the right column.

Your sponsorship investment: $X.00

Sponsorship Package Benefit	*Fulfillment Report Details*
Summarize sold benefits	Summarize delivery details
_____	_____
_____	_____
_____	_____
_____	_____
Total value of benefits offered: $X.00	*Total value of benefits delivered:* $X.00

Valuation provided by the Partnership Group – Sponsorship Specialists™ <Insert name of company who performed your valuation>

In this summary section, it is essential to note the sponsor's cash and/or contra investment above the chart so they can refer to what they paid you directly. At the bottom of each column you need to also include the value of the benefits offered and delivered. (The value was determined during the valuation audit.)

It is essential to show this number so the sponsor can compare the value of benefits promised and the value of what was delivered to their investment. This is critical for their ROI analysis.

If you have an outside firm provide a valuation audit, you should have the exact value for each benefit offered and delivered. Once you have this information, it is important to provide clarity to the sponsor as well and indicate who performed the valuation audit so the sponsor can authenticate it if necessary.

SUMMARY AND RECOMMENDATIONS

Include a summary of the event and how it went, as well as recommendations for the sponsor's renewal, such as fewer tickets in the package, signage to arrive earlier, or new activation ideas. This demonstrates to the sponsor that you are thinking ahead about how their program can be even better.

APPENDIX

Include pages of scanned media pieces, photos of the event with their signage and people. If the material is on a flash drive or website link, summarize on this page what they will find.

Enclosed you will find:

> Photos of event activities (4)
> Photos of your signage on display as per contract (12)
> Photo of your staff and clients in reception tent
> Photo of your president addressing the audience
> Copies of our print ads with your logo inclusion (5)
> In the pocket, a DVD that includes the radio commercials and
  TV commercials (12 of each) with your logo / name recognition
> Other materials

> **EXERCISE**
> *Use the sample template to create a fulfillment report for a sponsored event, program or property with which you are familiar. Invent details as needed.*

TO SUM UP

It is not enough to deliver everything you promised and more, or to go above and beyond to make up for something you could not deliver. You have to communicate all of that to the sponsor promptly and clearly. A fulfillment report within a month of the sponsorship's final moments demonstrates your sponsor's ROI, reinforces your relationship and sets you up for a discussion about renewing and improving the sponsorship.

SPONSOR
SUMMITS

REALITY CHECK – THE SPONSOR THANK-YOU PARTY IS AS BAD AS THE CHRISTMAS COCKTAIL CIRCUIT.

REALITY
CHECK

So many properties hold their traditional "sponsor thank you party." But much of the motivation is social rather than actually helping the sponsor. You need to differentiate and deliver value to your sponsor, not another rubber chicken thank-you dinner!

A sponsor summit brings sponsors together to look at ways to activate and leverage their sponsorships, make business-to-business connections and learn more about the opportunities available from the property.

Sponsor summits are an important part of relationship-building between sponsors and properties as well as sponsors and sponsors. When done right, they ensure long-term partners. Be sure you deliver value... not just another game of golf.

Your sponsors have several things in common. The most obvious one, of course, is that they sponsor your property. That tells you some other things about them:

> Since sponsorship is a means to their achieve business objectives, they need to execute sponsorship as well as possible.
> They need your audience as customers, fans or advocates.
> They could potentially do even more with you, and they want to, but they need help to imagine what "more" would look like.

By bringing your sponsors together in a carefully planned session guided by the needs they share, you can help them work more effectively with you, find synergies that boost their effectiveness with you, and even contribute to their overall business success. Imagine the goodwill that would result from a summit like that! The event that can achieve all this for you and your sponsors is a "sponsor summit." In this section, you will learn the elements of hosting and benefitting from sponsor summits: what they are, why you and your sponsors need them, how to plan them, and how to reap their long-term benefits.

14
MAKING YOUR SPONSOR SUMMIT
A "CAN'T MISS" EVENT

Above all, a sponsor summit is a chance for you and your partners to develop business – new business among themselves and new business with you. Sponsors should leave your summit with new contacts and leads as well as new ideas about sponsorship and activation for all of their sponsorships, not just those with you. (By now, we hope you have realized that there is no room for selfishness in the sponsorship business!)

When you imagine bringing your partners together, especially if the sponsorships have been successful, your first thought may be a thank-you party replete with opportunities for your sponsors to kick back and enjoy themselves.

Stop right there! Your sponsors' calendars are already full of business-related must-do parties and golf tournaments that impinge on their dwindling professional and personal moments – none of them meaningful, none of them memorable and all boasting hospitality budgets larger than yours.

Instead, offer something that sets you apart from your competitors and the companies that want to party with your sponsors. Offer them a productive learning event that will generate new business. Plan to present something – an expert speaker on an emerging trend, your next headline event entertainers, some critical information or "first news" about your property – that will make your sponsors want to attend.

The Saskatchewan Roughriders used a sponsor summit to feed their sponsors insider information. Before the summit, the Roughriders' mascot, Gainer the Gopher, had been banned from the Calgary Stampeders' stadium just before a playoff game there. At the dinner that ended the summit, the Roughriders' president announced that the "crisis" had been resolved and Gainer would be at the stadium after all. The sponsors received the news before it was released to the media – a gesture that underlined how valuable they were to the Roughriders organization.

If you have observed some weaknesses in your sponsors' activation tactics, you can use a sponsor summit to educate sponsors. Bring in a knowledgeable guest speaker to guide them in better activation with your property, and help them discover how to work with one another to lift their activation to an even higher level.

Strengthening relationships and helping your sponsors work better with you are just two of many potential outcomes of a well-planned sponsorship summit. Picture two of your sponsors discovering a hugely profitable new business opportunity with each other. That happened one year at a NASCAR sponsor summit. Coca Cola was present and so was Simon Malls, the world's largest owner/ operator of shopping malls. After meeting at the summit, the sponsorship staff of the two companies created Coca Cola's exclusive sponsorship with Simon, which called for every food court at every Simon mall to serve only Coca Cola beverage brands. In return, Coca Cola leveraged its sponsorship of American Idol to arrange for the show's regional tryouts to be held at Simon malls for two years.

Opportunities like those can be replicated at every level. Even small charities can create something similar for small business sponsors. Such a summit makes you stand out among a myriad of sponsorship hopefuls.

Now you are beginning to understand how your property will benefit from a sponsor summit that is not a party. Do not mix it with any other event or purpose such as making it part of the sponsored event. You want to set it apart and set the stage to do more with your sponsors individually and together.

ORGANIZING YOUR SUMMIT – SETTING GOALS AND OBJECTIVES
What do you want the summit to achieve, both for you and for your sponsors? A clear idea of goals and objectives for your sponsors and your own property will help you plan an effective experience for everyone.

It is important to understand that there are two sets of objectives when you hold a summit: your objectives (internal) and the objectives for your sponsors (external). You need to determine what your internal objectives are. At the same time you need to provide value for your sponsors, so there also must be measurable objectives for them.

If you believe that your sponsorships were weakened by a lack of activation, or if you have heard that from your sponsors, then a better understanding of activation could be a significant internal goal for a summit. It might even be the only one you need, especially for the first time. How can you help your sponsors grasp the difference that activation makes, and who can you bring in to explain that to them? How can your sponsor-partners help you raise your revenues? Can they sell tickets? Can they work together on joint activation tactics?

Getting feedback might also be a helpful internal goal. If you choose that, be sure to structure the session carefully, perhaps with the help of a facilitator and note-taker. Wide open "tell us what you think" sessions seldom elicit concrete strategies that can be implemented for immediate benefit. We never recommend introducing this approach at your first summit.

Give yourself permission to ask for help from your sponsors if you need it. If you would like more sponsors, your goal might be to obtain one new sponsorship prospect lead from each sponsor attending. If your sponsors have strong brands, you might ask them to share ideas for making your brand stronger, based on their own expertise and their experience with your property. If sponsorship is a core revenue source for your property, then it makes sense to seek sponsor input into your strategic plan.

As you can see, you will have no trouble setting your internal goals for a sponsor summit. Your only challenge might be to narrow your list so that you have a manageable number for the time frame you have chosen. Three or four are usually enough, and if your summit is short – just a couple of hours – you will only need one.

It is just as important to have a clear idea of the goals for your sponsors, for those external goals will be the foundation of the pitch that motivates them to attend. Set your external goals with one question in mind: What develops business for your sponsors?

Send the message that the summit will show your sponsors some of the other areas where you can assist all of them beyond what you are selling them now. Perhaps you want every one of them to meet two new partners, or achieve a business deal together that has nothing to do with you, or do all their sponsorships – not just yours – better. And remember to talk to your sponsors about what they believe they need from such an event.

> **EXERCISE**
> *Using a property with which you are familiar, set three internal*
> *goals for its sponsor summit and three external goals that benefit*
> *the sponsors.*

TIMING AND ATTENDEES

Talk to key sponsors about a good time of year and an appropriate date. If you are able to get lead sponsors to commit even before you send out invitations, their participation will attract your other sponsors. While larger organizations hold a sponsor summit every year, smaller organizations may find that every two or three years is enough. Be mindful of the busy periods in your sponsors' business cycles as you set the date.

As you plan your summit, tailor it to the highest-ranking people you can possibly attract from your sponsors' staff. Those people are busy. Their time is precious. They will think twice about any commitment that includes significant travel time. They can always arrange social and recreational opportunities for themselves with the people they prefer, so keep your summit short, focused on learning and tightly scheduled. A short summit packed with meaningful content is better than a longer one that drags.

Half a day or even two hours may suffice. If you plan for a full day, allow suitable travel time before and afterwards. If you plan for a day and a half, make every mo-ment count and be sure to include accommodation.

Take your summit off-site. When your summit is in your building, there are too many internal distractions for you and your staff. Sponsors may be sidetracked as well. With an overnight summit, take it right out of your market area to ensure that you have the complete attention of your sponsors and staff for the full summit. Neither sponsors nor staff can quickly "run back to the office" to take care of some-thing, returning late or not at all. It also allows the sponsors to build relationships with one other.

It may be appropriate to divide your sponsors for part of the summit. Single-year and multiple-year sponsors may have different goals for themselves and different levels of experience with your property. Or perhaps they are drawn from two markedly different business sectors, business-to-business and business-to-consumer, for example. In such cases, a pre- or post-summit session for each might be helpful and more effective for their goals.

A WORD ABOUT BUDGETS

The property is the host, so the property pays for everything, including accommodation if the summit lasts more than a day. This gives you the right to invite specific people – which will allow you to approach more senior staff members, and to keep the overall number down to a level that ensures meaningful participation for everyone.

Start building the costs into future sponsorship packages, perhaps by adding 10% for the summit. (Remember, your proposal does not include a breakdown of individual costs, just the market value of your assets.)

You can also reduce the cash costs of the sponsor summit by turning it into one more opportunity for sponsorship. With a guest list of businesspeople who host their own corporate events from time to time, you should be able to get sponsors for the summit venue and food.

WHAT CONTENT DO YOU NEED?

Like your sponsorship proposal and the sponsorship itself, the summit is not about you. It is about your sponsors – what they need and what they can learn. As you plan your agenda, look at every content idea through your sponsors' eyes.

The more your sponsors know about each other, the more effectively they will be able to find synergies and work together to build better sponsorships. If your partners do not know one another well, consider an icebreaker session where they meet and hear about one another's business objectives. This can help them generate better ideas during the rest of the summit.

If you have already planned your media campaign for the next event in which sponsors may be involved, the summit offers an ideal opportunity to present it. Step back from the limelight and ask your media partners, rather than your own marketing people or your media agency, to run the session. Be sure to include ideas on how sponsors will be able to leverage your media campaign to meet their goals.

Your partners deserve to hear exciting details, so sharing news before releasing it to the public demonstrates how much you value your sponsors. Have you secured a celebrity or headline entertainer? Did you create a new promotional or commemorative product for your property? Are you planning to enhance or change your event or property in other ways? Tell your sponsors first at the summit.

Perhaps you and your sponsors have experienced some logistical bumps in the road during activation. Signage in particular can be a source of misunderstanding. Pass out your graphics standards package and explain it. Talk about its expectations for appearance and materials and its policies on signage and banner placement. By sharing these details with all sponsors at the same time, you demonstrate that your policies are consistent and fairly applied. You may also receive helpful feedback about changes to specifications that would work better for your sponsors without impeding your own goals. Such frank dialogue strengthens your relationship with your sponsors.

Activation, no matter how terrific, can always be improved. The possibilities are endless. A session on activation opportunities and how they may work for you and your sponsors is always valuable. If some sponsors have activated particularly well with your property or others, invite them to join a panel discussion so they can share their experiences with all partners. Then have a conversation on how your partners might find synergies by working together on their sponsorships. If possible, include past sponsors who have been particularly successful at activation. Do not let a relationship lapse just because you are not doing business with them this year.

Finally, if you have been listening to your sponsors during your relationship, you may have heard about a business challenge common to all of them: keeping up with growing mobile use, for example, or maintaining effective HR processes in small businesses without an HR professional on staff. Bring in a guest speaker who addresses these challenges meaningfully, and you will give your sponsors something they have not found anywhere else.

In short, the content is what makes your meeting. Again, this is a business summit, not a social event, so you do not need to worry about providing a memorable menu. For a two-hour event, snacks afterwards are enough. If your summit takes a full day or runs overnight, you will need to feed people appropriately, but not extravagantly.

BE SURE TO FOLLOW UP

Have you ever been to a dinner party where the host sent you a thank-you note? Here's more proof that a sponsor summit is not a social event: You are going to send thank-you notes to your sponsors for coming to your summit!

That's right. They trusted you enough to assume that your summit would be worthwhile and well-planned. They found time in their busy schedules to attend. They devoted several hours to something that strengthened their relationship with you. That is commitment – and commitment deserves to be acknowledged.

We hope that the notion of a merged form letter did not enter your mind even for a moment. These notes should be personal and use the words *you* and *your* more often than I (and when you use *we* or *our*, you should be talking about you and the sponsor, not your organization). Here is an example:

> *Dear Mary,*
>
> *Your participation in the Heritage Theatre's Sponsor Summit means a great deal to me. I am grateful for everything that Sensational Shoes has helped us to achieve so far, and excited about how the theatre might bring you even greater value in the future.*
>
> *I especially appreciated your (here you can highlight Mary's key point during a discussion, her warm welcome to a first-time sponsor, or an example of successful activation that she shared). Thank you for helping to make our Sponsor Summit better by (sharing your experiences, ideas etc.) with our other partners.*
>
> *You can expect to hear from me soon with a summary of discussions, conclusions and action items from the summit. And as always, your suggestions and questions are most welcome at any time.*
>
> *Sincerely,*
> *Patrick*

Then, of course, follow up with that summit report. Think of it as being similar to a fulfillment report. Its purpose is to communicate about action items and demonstrate completion. It also gives you one more touch point with the sponsors you value. Finally, if you have planned your summit carefully, the report reminds sponsors of a summit that succeeded.

CASE STUDY

Grant MacEwan University in Edmonton and Funtastic in Vernon, BC planned summits focused on their sponsors instead of themselves. They said from the outset that sponsors were there to learn and understand how they could make better sponsorship investments in the future. They informed the sponsors that the events were not solely about their investments with MacEwan or Funtastic, but their overall investment in sponsorship. They expressed the hope that sponsors would leave with knowledge they could apply to other sponsorships, not just these two.

At the Funtastic event, sponsors approached the Funtastic team and said, "Is this really a smart move? You are educating us on how to be more effective and do better deals. We may ask you for more than we are getting now!"

Executive director **Jim McEwan** replied, "I would rather you understand sponsorship and make better overall investments to grow your business in this marketplace than just get your money." That was definitely the right answer.

Both properties held their summits off site. The Funtastic event was at the River City Casino in Vernon, which went above and beyond to ensure everything went smoothly. The food was simple, but extremely tasty and elegantly presented. The Casino marketing and operations staff attended to learn more about sponsorship. At the MacEwan event, the atmosphere was casual. The Edmonton Marriott at

River Cree Resort reconfigured both the meeting and lunch rooms into amazing spaces. The main summit room was decked out with casual chairs and couches for an inviting, laid-back atmosphere. The lunch room was decorated in an African safari motif. Both rooms vividly illustrated how you can truly activate a hosting opportunity for sponsors.

The MacEwan event integrated a current sponsor's presentation about how and why her company invested in the sponsorship. She went on to describe their process to activate on the sponsorship and ultimately how they measured success. It was excellent for other sponsors to hear firsthand from a peer sponsor how to make things work.

Both events focused on sponsors, and both properties were successful in having sponsors leave with vastly increased knowledge. At the summits, both organizations were able to move forward with enhanced sponsorships.

Their goal was to educate, and they did. They demonstrated how they were truly partners with their sponsors and the sponsors reciprocated by saying, "You are the organization I want to do business with."

(Partnership Group – Sponsorship Specialists™ blog, December 14, 2010)

To sum up, here are four key principles for an effective sponsor summit:
> Determine clear objectives;
> Ensure that it is a working event with worthwhile outcomes;
> Tailor it carefully to your needs and the needs of your sponsors; and,
> Follow up afterwards.

15
REALITY: BETTER THAN YOU'D HOPED

Sponsorship is more than hanging a sign or posting a logo. We hope that through this book you have truly had a reality check! Whether you are a seasoned veteran or a student interested in a career in the industry, there are some basics to remember. Sponsorship is not complicated. You now have all the tools to be successful. The key is to remember a few crucial points.

SPONSORSHIP IS A FORM OF MARKETING

It is an experiential marketing channel that delivers results and allows brands to reach and engage with their focused target audience. Like the relationship between the sponsor and its target audience, the relationship between the property and the brand takes time to develop and nurture. Sponsorship is not a matter of putting together a stock package and pitching it. Rather, it means learning about your prospects, understanding their needs, cultivating strong, trust-based relationships and delivering custom proposals and programs that specifically meet their needs.

YOU ACHIEVE SUCCESS BY HAVING THE RIGHT TOOLS
>   Knowing what you have to sell and what those assets are worth;
>   Prospecting correctly and doing discovery sessions;
>   Creating custom-built programs for prospects and then fulfilling on the programs when sold.

You nurture sponsor relationships through steady, creative activation support and meaningful sponsor summits.

But no matter how great your tools, the true reality check is that **unless you have built and maintained each relationship, you will not achieve lasting success with sponsorship.**

Thank you for reading and may you be truly successful.

GLOSSARY

Activation: the marketing activities a company conducts to leverage its sponsorship. The money spent on activation is over and above the rights fee paid to the sponsored property.

Ambush marketing: a promotional strategy that takes place around a sponsorship property by a non-sponsor (often a competitor to the official sponsor) but does not involve payment of a sponsorship fee to the event. The ambush marketer attempts to capitalize on the popularity/prestige of a property by giving the false impression that it is a sponsor without paying any rights fees.

Arts marketing: a promotional strategy linking a company to the visual or performing arts (sponsorship of a symphony concert series or museum exhibit, for example).

Assets: Those elements owned by a property and of worth to a sponsor that the property can sell the sponsor to achieve their goals and objectives. Assets comprise a property's inventory.

BATNA: an acronym meaning "best alternative to a negotiated agreement," coined by Roger Gisher and William Ury in their 1981 bestseller, Getting to Yes: Negotiating Without Giving In.

Benefits: a synonym for Assets.

Brand: see Sponsorship/Sponsorship buyer.

Brand experience: a 3D advertising program (a multi-faceted, experiential program) developed in a way that includes and engages the consumer.

Bundling: combining several assets or benefits from the inventory to make a package or proposal for a sponsor. Bundling, as opposed to selling à la carte or as individual benefits in a "one off" fashion, is the most effective way to generate maximum dollars for a property and deliver the best return on investment (ROI) for a sponsor.

Business-to-business (B2B) sponsorship: a program intended to influence corporate rather than individual consumer awareness and behaviour.

Buzz marketing: a low- or no-cost method of viral marketing using word of mouth that has people telling other people about a company's products or services.

Category exclusivity: a sponsor's right to be the only company within its product or service category associated with the sponsored property.

Cause marketing or Cause-related marketing: a type of marketing involving the cooperative efforts of a for-profit business and a nonprofit organization for mutual benefit. The term is sometimes used more broadly and generally to refer to any type of marketing effort for social and other charitable causes, including in-house marketing efforts by nonprofit organizations. It generally includes an offer by the sponsor to make a donation to the cause with purchase of its product or service. Cause marketing differs from corporate giving (philanthropy) in that the latter generally involves a specific donation that is tax deductible, while cause marketing is a business expense and is expected to show a return on investment.

Co-sponsors: sponsors of the same property.

Cost/benefit ratio: a ratio that attempts to summarize the overall dollar value of a project or proposal that a sponsor expects for each dollar it invests in rights fees. Cross-promotions: joint marketing efforts conducted by two or more co-sponsors leveraging the sponsored property.

CSR (corporate social responsibility): a concept whereby companies manage the business processes to produce an overall positive impact on society, by taking responsibility for the impact of their activities on customers, employees, shareholders, communities and the environment in all aspects of their operations.

Discovery or exploratory session: an initial meeting or meetings with a prospect to determine needs, goals and objectives so that the property can build a customized proposal to deliver on these needs and ultimately show a positive return on investment for the sponsor. This is the initial stage in the sponsorship development process once a prospect has been determined.

Event marketing: a promotional strategy linking a company to a special event (sponsorship of a sports competition, festival, etc.) to support corporate objectives. Often used as a synonym for "sponsorship." The latter term is preferable, however, because not all sponsorships involve an event.

Experiential marketing: connecting face-to-face with your target user by offering an engaging, entertaining and interactive brand experience that is unmatched by traditional advertising.

Fulfillment: delivery of benefits promised to the sponsor in the contract.

Guerilla marketing: a promotional strategy that uses unconventional marketing intended to get maximum results from minimal resources. Guerilla marketing can be as different from traditional marketing as guerilla warfare is from traditional warfare. Rather than marching their marketing dollars forth like infantry divisions, guerilla marketers snipe away with their marketing resources for maximum impact. Hospitality: the hosting of key customers, clients, government officials, employees and other VIPs at an event. It can involve tickets, parking, dining and other amenities, often in a specially designated area.

In-kind sponsorship: payment (full or partial) of the sponsorship fee in goods or services rather than cash.

Intangible benefits: "soft" benefits that are hard to measure but important to capture.

Integrated marketing communications (IMC): an approach that says the effects of one marketing method cannot be considered in isolation from other marketing methods, and that synergy is a critical strategic component.

Inventory: the complete catalogue of all physical and non-physical assets or benefits that may be made available to sponsorship buyers. The inventory (if fully delivered) should indicate all benefits and assets, their real market value, their fulfillment cost to deliver, and the overall value of the inventory.

Licensed merchandise: goods produced by a manufacturer (the licensee) who has obtained a license to produce and distribute a property's official marks on products such as clothing and souvenirs.

MARCOM (sometimes spelled "marcomm"): an abbreviation for "marketing communications." Marcom is targeted interaction with customers and prospects using one or more media, such as direct mail, newspapers and magazines, television, radio, billboards, telemarketing and the Internet.

Mark: any official visual representation of a property, including emblems and mascots.

Media sponsor: the media partner that provides either cash, or usually advertising time or space, to a property in exchange for that designation.

Mnemonic: an audio memory aid (such as a musical cue like Intel's four notes) often used in advertising.

Option to renew: the contractual right to renew a sponsorship on specified terms. Pass-through rights: benefits that the property allows a sponsor to transfer to another company, provided that company is not a competitor to another property sponsor. For example, Molson may wish to pass through some rink board signage at a Leafs game to a local bar with which it does business, and in return gain more pouring taps at the establishment.

Philanthropy: an idea, event, or action that is done to for the benefit of humanity and usually involves some sacrifice rather than a profit motive. Acts of philanthropy include donating money to a charity, volunteering at a local shelter, or raising money to donate to a cause.

Philanthropic gift: as defined by Canada Revenue Agency, a cash and/or in-kind contribution given to a registered charity by an individual, company, foundation or organization without any expectation of anything, including recognition, in return, or without receipt of any benefits that have a market value greater than 10% of the gift to a maximum of $75.

GLOSSARY

Presenting sponsor: the sponsor that has its name presented just above or below that of the sponsored property. A "presenting" sponsor differs from a "title" sponsor as the event name and the Sponsor name are not fully integrated; for example, "The Skins Game Presented by Telus" versus "Telus Skins Game."

Primary sponsor: the sponsor that pays the largest fee and in return receives the most property benefits if the property has no title or presenting sponsor.

Property: an entity, event or vehicle that offers brands the opportunity to deepen their relationship with their target consumers, thereby helping to achieve the brands' business objectives.

Proposal: the presentation that outlines the property and the objectives of the sponsor, and lists benefits that the sponsor will receive to achieve its objectives in exchange for a specified investment in cash or in-kind.

Prospect: a company or organization that a property has qualified to be a sponsor based on research and indications that the property's assets fit with the company's business objectives.

Return on investment (ROI): the measurement sponsors or buyers use to determine if their investment in a specific property was good or not. It traditionally measures against such metrics as brand loyalty, brand awareness, traffic, sales leads, actual sales, employee morale, community awareness or other elements based on the sponsors' reasons for investing.

Right of first refusal: a sponsor's contractual right to match any offer the property receives from a competitor in the sponsor's defined product category during a specific period of time.

Rights fee: the payment (cash or in-kind) made by a sponsor to a property.

Sales rights: a sponsor's preferred supplier right to sell its product or service to the property or its attendees or members.

Signage: banners, billboards, electronic messages, etc., displayed on site and containing sponsor ID.

Sponsee: a property available for sponsorship.

Sponsor (or sponsorship buyer): the payer of a fee to the owner of a property for the purpose of gaining commercial rights related to the property. To sponsor something is to support an event, activity, person or organization by providing money or other resources in exchange for something, usually advertising or publicity, and always access to an audience.

Sponsorship: a cash and/or in-kind fee paid to a property (typically in sports, arts, education, health, entertainment or causes) in return for the exploitable commercial potential associated with that property.

Sponsorship fee: see Rights fee.

Sponsorship marketing: the activation or leveraging of a sponsorship beyond the usual advertising, publicity and audience access.

Stealth marketing: any practice designed to deceive people about the involvement of marketers in a communication.

Strategic philanthropy: the practice of using philanthropic funds to create social and brand value.

Street (level) marketing: marketing activities undertaken by a member of a psychographic niche to further the adoption of an idea, goods or service by that niche.

Supplier: the official provider of goods or services in exchange for designated recognition. This level is below official sponsor, and the benefits provided are limited accordingly.

Tangible benefits: concrete benefits that are easy to measure.

Title sponsor: the sponsor that has its name incorporated into the name of the sponsored property; e.g., "Telus Skins Game."

Value: the real market worth of a property asset or package. These values are calculated by industry accepted standards and represent the individual value of each benefit or the bundled value of the proposal. It is not the same thing as price. The price or investment is usually 10-15% lower than the actual value of the proposal.

Venue marketing: a promotional strategy linking a sponsor to a physical site such as stadiums, arenas, auditoriums, amphitheaters, racetracks or fairgrounds.

Virtual signage: the electronic insertion of signage that is not actually present at the event during a TV broadcast.

BONUS
MATERIALS

INVENTORY VALUATION AND COSTING TEMPLATE

INVENTORY LISTS – VALUES – TIERS
TIER ONE – $150,000+
TIER TWO – $100,000 TO $150,000
TIER THREE – $50,000 TO $100,000
TIER FOUR – $25,000 TO $50,000
TIER FIVE – $15,000 TO $25,000
TIER SIX – $5,000 TO $15,000
TIER SEVEN – UNDER $5,000

PRODUCT	DESCRIPTION	VALUE OF BENEFIT	PROJECTED SPONSOR COST	# AVAIL	# SOLD	# LEFT
		$0.00	$0.00	0	0	0
		$0.00	$0.00	0	0	0
		$0.00	$0.00	0	0	0
		$0.00	$0.00	0	0	0
		$0.00	$0.00	0	0	0
		$0.00	$0.00	0	0	0
		$0.00	$0.00	0	0	0
		$0.00	$0.00	0	0	0
		$0.00	$0.00	0	0	0

TOTAL COSTS ESTIMATED
TOTAL REVENUE POTENTIAL

(Copyright of The Barootes Partnership Group Inc. 2002)

TOTAL SPONSOR COST	GROSS REVENUE	PROPERTY COST PER	PROPERTY TOTAL COST	NET REVENUE POTENTIAL	TIER ELIGIBILITY
$0.00	$0.00	$0.00	$0.00	$0.00	
$0.00	$0.00	$0.00	$0.00	$0.00	
$0.00	$0.00	$0.00	$0.00	$0.00	
$0.00	$0.00	$0.00	$0.00	$0.00	
$0.00	$0.00	$0.00	$0.00	$0.00	
$0.00	$0.00	$0.00	$0.00	$0.00	
$0.00	$0.00	$0.00	$0.00	$0.00	
$0.00	$0.00	$0.00	$0.00	$0.00	
$0.00	$0.00	$0.00	$0.00	$0.00	
$0.00			**$0.00**		
	$0.00			**$0.00**	

INVENTORY EVALUATION MATRIX

The following is the inventory asset pricing structure that the Partnership Group – Sponsorship Specialists™ uses to establish fair market values for assets in an inventory. This pricing structure is a guideline only and not to be deemed as applicable to all properties at all times. Depending on a specific property at any given time the value of assets may be more than projected here or less than illustrated depending on the uniqueness of the asset and the property.

SAMPLING OPPORTUNITY VALUATION

Is the sampling product being handed out to a non-focused audience or without face-to-face interaction?

Is the sampling product being handed out to a targeted audience, with face-to-face interaction?

TICKETS AND HOSPITALITY VALUATION

The tickets have a face value and are for a venue that delivers greater than 70% capacity

The tickets have a face value and are for a venue that delivers less than 70% capacity

The tickets have no face value

The tickets are VIP passes or accreditation

SAMPLE VALUE	SAMPLING OPPORTUNITY VALUE
$0.05/sample	Number of people sampled x sample value
$0.20/sample	Number of people sampled x sample value

TICKET VALUE	TICKET AND HOSPITALITY OPPORTUNITY VALUE
Face value	Ticket face value x number of tickets
Face value	Ticket face value x capacity percentage x number of tickets
Value of the general benefits received at the event ÷ the number of guests	Ticket calculated value x number of tickets
Regular ticket price plus 10% – 500% mark-up	Premium ticket price x number of tickets

INVENTORY EVALUATION MATRIX... *continued*

MAILING LIST VALUATION

Is the mailing list a compilation (collection of multiple other lists) or available from other sources such as an association?

Is the list NOT a compilation (a focused list) or NOT available from other sources?

SPONSOR ID IN MEASURED MEDIA VALUATION

Is the sponsor media mention limited to logo only or just a mention?
Is clutter evident?

Does the media mention include multiple logos or highlighted mention or limited clutter (i.e.: presenting sponsor)?

Is the media inclusion (space, time etc) for the sole and full use of the sponsor?

SPONSOR ID IN NON-MEASURED MEDIA VALUATION

Property Publications
Is the logo/ID located on a "sponsor page" with other sponsors inside the publication?

Is the logo/ID featured on its own on the cover or back of the publication?

Is the mention an advertisement in the publication?

NAME VALUE	MAILING LIST VALUE
$0.05/name	Number of names x name value
$0.20/name	Number of names x name value

MENTION VALUE	MEDIA MENTION OPPORTUNITY VALUE
5% of retail media cost x percentage (¼, ½ or all) of the of total media package exposure	Mention value as calculated
10% of retail media cost x percentage (¼, ½ or all) of the of total media package exposure	Mention value as calculated
100% of retail media cost/value	Mention value as calculated

MENTION VALUE	MEDIA MENTION OPPORTUNITY VALUE
$0.00325/logo or mention	Mention value x number of publications printed
$0.025 – $0.065/logo or mention	Mention value x number of publications printed
Rate card values or $0.00325 – $0.065/ mention or advertisement	Mention value x number of publications printed

INVENTORY EVALUATION MATRIX... *continued*

SPONSOR ID IN NON-MEASURED MEDIA VALUATION... *continued*

Tickets
Is the logo/ID located with other sponsor logos/IDs?
Is the logo/ID featured with few other logos or on its own?
Is the logo/ID associated with a ticket back coupon opportunity?
Is the ticket for an event that would be considered a collector's item?

Websites
Is the mention a logo/ID located on a "sponsor page"?
Is the logo/ID featured on the website or located on a specialized website with a targeted audience?
Is the logo/ID a part of a banner or pop-up, etc. on the website?

Is the mention a featured article on the website that includes sponsors logo/ID and product descriptions?

Program Schedules
Is the logo/ID located on a program schedule for a one-day event?
Is the logo/ID located with other sponsor logos/IDs?
Is the logo/ID featured on its own on the cover or back of the publication?
Is the logo/ID located on the program schedule for the duration of the season?

MEASURED MEDIA ADVERTISING VALUATION

Static Signage
Is the logo/ID on signage along with other sponsor logos/IDs?
Is the signage located at a one-time event?
Is the logo/ID featured on signage on its own, featured prominently or on signage that will appear for a longer period of time?
Is the signage located at an event where attendance is expected to be below 70%?

MENTION VALUE	MEDIA MENTION OPPORTUNITY VALUE
$0.00325/ticket	Mention value x number of tickets printed
$0.00325 – $0.04/ticket	Mention value x number of tickets printed
$0.04 – $0.065/ticket	Mention value x number of tickets printed
$0.04 – $0.065/ticket	Mention value x number of tickets printed
$0.00325/unique user	Mention value x number of unique users
$0.00325 – $0.065/unique user	Mention value x number of unique users
Rate card values or $0.00325 – $0.065/unique user	Mention value x number of unique users
$0.13/unique user	Mention value x number of unique users
$0.00325/logo or mention	Mention value x number of printed schedules
$0.00325/logo or mention	Mention value x number of printed schedules
$0.00325 – $0.013/logo or mention	Mention value x number of printed schedules
$0.013 – $0.065/logo or mention	Mention value x number of printed schedules

MENTION VALUE	ADVERTISING OPPORTUNITY VALUE
$0.00325/logo	Mention value x number of attendees/viewers
$0.00325/logo	Mention value x number of attendees/viewers
$0.00325 – $0.026/logo	Mention value x number of attendees/viewers
As above	Mention value x attendance percentage x number of attendees/viewers

INVENTORY EVALUATION MATRIX... *continued*

MEASURED MEDIA ADVERTISING VALUATION... *continued*

Electronic Logos or Moving Signage
Is the logo/ID on signage along with other sponsor logos/IDs?

Is the signage located at a one-time event?

Is the logo/ID featured on signage on its own, featured prominently or on signage that will appear for a longer period of time?
Is the signage located at an event where attendance is expected to be below 70%?

Jumbotron Advertisement
Advertisements on a Jumbotron or multiple screen TVs, based on 30-second commercial space

PA Announcements
Is the announcement a name mention or included with other sponsors?

Is the announcement accompanied with a sell line or worked into the performance?

Does the announcement include a speaking opportunity for the sponsor?

MENTION VALUE	ADVERTISING OPPORTUNITY VALUE
$0.00325/logo	Mention value x number of attendees/ viewers x number of views
$0.00325/logo	Mention value x number of attendees/ viewers x number of views
$0.00325 – $0.026/logo	Mention value x number of attendees/ viewers x number of views
As above	Mention value x attendance percentage x number of attendees/viewers x number of views
$0.04/logo or advertisement	Mention value x number of viewers x number of ads
$0.00325/mention	Mention value x number of mentions x number of attendees
$0.065/mention	Mention value x number of mentions x number of attendees
$0.065/mention	Mention value x number of mentions x number of attendees

SMALLVILLE COMMUNITY RECREATION CENTRE

NAMING RIGHTS SPONSORSHIP PROPOSAL

PREPARED FOR:
ACME FINANCIAL

PRESENTED BY:

PROJECT AT-A-GLANCE

FACILITY HIGHLIGHTS

As the regions only LEED's certified facility this "green" destination has proven to be a very sought-after commodity.

In just 11 months of operation it has already surpassed attendance estimates by 143%, making it the busiest sports facility in the province. The 1,200,000 visitors have toured the facility and all it has to offer, specifically:

> Two NHL-sized arenas, each with seating for 250 persons
> Two indoor fieldhouses primarily for multipurpose dry sports, but also for other uses, including indoor soccer, food and banquet services, and seniors' lawn bowling
> Fitness and wellness centre with an indoor walking track, change rooms and support areas
> Leased spaces for complementary services and amenities such as sports stores, sports medicine and physiotherapy
> Family lounge to develop the social aspect of the facility, enhancing spontaneous passholder development and retention
> Additional administrative space and support sufficient to accommodate the added components, including an additional 538 parking spaces

Located at the juncture of the two most travelled highways in the region, it is visible to over 2,500,000 vehicles annually.

Combined with a strategic sponsorship program that will limit the number of partners and manage the "clutter," as well as promote to a demonstrated active digital media audience of over 470,000, the Recreation Centre is ripe to be "owned."

OUR MEETING RECAP

In this section insert a recap of ideally one to three pages of your discovery meeting(s) (as outlined earlier).

This should include:

> a thank-you for their interest
> a recap of what was learned, such as goals, objectives, budget etc.
> a few lines about how this program was designed to specifically meet their objectives: how the benefits they will receive as outlined in the following pages will assist them to achieve the goals and objectives noted in the previous page
> A final thank-you and a statement that this is a "draft proposal" that can be further fine-tuned to meet their specific needs
> This should be custom-written for each presentation. ***Remember, this is all about the prospect and not you!!***

THE PARTNERSHIP OPPORTUNITY

Set the pace and the example with your brand identifying and naming the most leading-edge, comprehensive recreation facility in Ontario.

This unique branding platform will not only create "live life" experiences for your target audience but also knit your company into the fabric of the community. Thousands of visitors, teams, and families will use the facility on a daily basis year-round.

As the Title Naming Rights holder to the entire new venue, (i.e. "The ACME Financial Centre"), ACME Financial will be extended the following.

RIGHTS AND BENEFITS:

1. EXCLUSIVITY
Industry Event and Category Exclusivity; The City will provide ACME Financial with industry category exclusivity in the following partnership category with regard to other companies' participation within the new facility (Centre): ACME Financial category; No other competitive company in the defined category will be permitted to participate in the facility as a sponsor, nor will they be able to sponsor any new centre events.

2. TRADEMARKS AND LOGOS
The City will work with ACME Financial to create a new combination Centre logo and provide ACME Financial with the resultant Centre trademarks and logos that are specific to the facility in electronic format for reproduction and display by ACME FINANCIAL during the term of the partnership, for the purposes of promoting, marketing, and advertising the participation of ACME Financial in the Centre.

3. PAID MEDIA ADVERTISING

The City will include the Centre logo as contemplated above in its entire paid media buy, such as paid newspaper, magazine and/or internet advertising as well as any outdoor or television campaigns if conducted. The identified media at this time includes the following:

Publications/Marketing Collateral Materials

> ACME Financial will be provided one full page advertising in each of the centre **spring/fall program guides** (2 full pages in total).
> (Estimated to be $255,000 per year). * *See page 171*

> ACME Financial will be provided logo inclusion on the front **cover of the centre spring/fall program guides.***

> ACME Financial will be provided logo inclusion on the **sponsor page of each of the program guides**.*

> ACME Financial will be provided with the opportunity for **customized editorial** of approximately 75 to 100 words in each of the program guides.*

> ACME Financial will be provided logo inclusion on the **front cover of any of the program or centre brochures printed.***
> (Estimated to be $120,000 per year).*

> ACME Financial will be provided logo inclusion on the front cover (masthead) of the **Centre newsletter.*** (Estimated to be $120,000 per year).

> ACME Financial will be provided logo inclusion on the **Centre letterhead.**

Other On-site Media

> ACME Financial will be provided with the opportunity to run **two 60-second commercials** per day (or time equivalent) on two TV flat screens at each entrance (existing and new entrance) to the Centre.*

> ACME Financial will be provided with the opportunity to run a corporate video of up to two minutes play (maximum 1 hour total play) per day on a continuous rotational basis on two TV flat screens at each entrance (existing and new entrance) to the Centre.*

> ACME Financial will be provided with the opportunity to run logo and naming identification and text messaging (max 30 seconds per message) on an outdoor digital corner parking lot display up to 12 times per 24-hour period.*

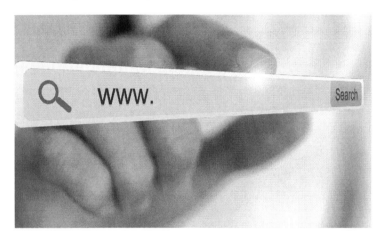

Centre Website

ACME Financial will be provided with logo and naming identification on the home page of the Centre website with a link back to the ACME FINANCIAL website for the term of the partnership.

ACME Financial will be provided with space for a 100-word profile regarding ACME and its support of the Centre on the Centre website for the term of the partnership.

ACME Financial will be provided with logo and naming identification on the Centre's dedicated sponsor web page with a link back to the ACME Financial website for the term of the partnership.

4. ON-SITE SIGNAGE

Building Signage – Outdoor
ACME Financial will be provided with logo and naming identification as the title sponsor of the Centre on the **outdoor building signage** at street level.

ACME Financial will be provided with logo and naming identification as the title sponsor of the Centre on the outdoor building signage on the south side of the building. (Minimum size 10' x 15')

ACME Financial will be identified as the title sponsor of the Centre on the **corner parking lot digital display sign** (display sign dimensions 35" x 20') with logo and naming identification.*

ACME Financial will be identified as the title sponsor of the Centre with logo and naming identification on the outdoor building welcome banner signage at the west and east entrances of the building.

ACME Financial will be identified as the title sponsor of the Centre with logo and naming identification on the landscape feature (currently forecast to be a waterfall feature) adjacent the main east entrance turn-around circle to the Centre.

A unique opportunity affording ACME Financial their company logo on the facility rooftop; specific signage details and application to be determined.

Building Signage – Indoor
i) Lobby and other public areas
ACME Financial will be provided with logo and naming identification as the title sponsor of the Centre on unique welcome signage in the form of hanging banners (size to be determined) in each entrance lobby area to the Centre.*

ACME Financial will be provided with logo and naming identification as the title sponsor of the Centre on a unique etched glass sponsor recognition sign in each entrance lobby area to the Centre.*

ACME Financial will be provided with logo and naming identification as the title sponsor of the Centre on carpet welcome signage in each entrance lobby area to the Centre.*

ACME Financial will be identified as the title sponsor of the Centre with logo and naming identification on all indoor directional signage in the Centre.

ACME Financial will be identified as the title sponsor of the Centre with logo and naming identification on all indoor pillar banner signage in the Centre. (12 -14 individual banners throughout the main corridor- size TBD)

ACME Financial will be identified as the title sponsor of the Centre with logo and naming identification on all facility podiums in the Centre as the title sponsor of the Centre.

ii) Arenas

ACME Financial will be identified as the title sponsor of the Centre with logo and naming identification on all three ice surfaces in the Centre with two in ice decals diagonally opposed between the centre ice line and the blueline (6 - six in total).

ACME Financial will be identified as the title sponsor of the Centre with logo and naming identification on both Olympia resurfacing machines in the Centre with a decal on one full side of the machine. (2 – two in total).

ACME Financial will be identified as the title sponsor of the Centre with logo and naming identification on 2 (two) rink boards per arena in the Centre with a board decal covered with lexan (6- six in total).*

ACME Financial will be identified as the title sponsor of the Centre with logo and naming identification with a decal on each arena scoreboard in the Centre (3 - three in total). *

ACME Financial will be identified as the title sponsor of the Centre with logo and naming identification on stair riser signage (one package of 12) per each arena .*

ACME Financial will be identified as the title sponsor of the Centre with logo and naming identification on one wall banner per arena. *

iii) Curling Rink

ACME Financial will be identified with logo and naming identification on one wall banner in the curling rink as the title sponsor of the Centre.*(minimum size 10' x 10')

ACME Financial will be identified with logo and naming identification on all eight ice surfaces in the curling Centre with an in ice decal as the title sponsor of the Centre (size TBD).*

ACME Financial will be provided with logo and naming identification on the etched glass doors of the curling rink as the centre title sponsor. *

ACME Financial will be provided with logo and naming identification on the etched glass windows of the lower and upper deck viewing areas of the curling rink as the centre title sponsor.*(12 windows per level)

ACME Financial will be provided with logo and naming identification on the Curling scoreboards of the curling rink as the centre title sponsor. *

ACME Financial will be provided with logo and naming identification on the Curling ceiling beams of the curling rink as the centre title sponsor.*

ACME Financial will be provided with logo and naming identification on the Curling lounge dividers of the curling rink as the centre title sponsor.*

iv) Aquatic Centre

ACME Financial will be identified as the title sponsor of the Centre with logo and naming identification on one large wall banner in the aquatic centre.*(minimum size 20' x 20')

ACME Financial will be identified as the title sponsor of the Centre with logo and naming identification on the waterslide in the aquatic centre.*(size TBD)

ACME Financial will be provided with logo and naming identification as the title sponsor of the Centre on the etched glass windows of the lower and upper deck viewing areas of the aquatic centre.*(12 windows per level)

v) Fieldhouse 1 – Soccer Field

ACME Financial will be identified as the title sponsor of the Centre with logo and naming identification in each change room with a 3' x 2' sign (4 - four in total).

ACME Financial will be identified with logo and naming identification as the title sponsor of the Centre on a wall banner on one of the main walls in the Centre Fieldhouse.

ACME Financial will be provided with logo and naming identification as the title sponsor of the Centre on the field scoreboards of the fieldhouse. *

ACME Financial will be identified with logo and naming identification as the title sponsor of the Centre on a end field wall on one end of the field of play in the Centre Fieldhouse. (Estimated size 80′ x 16′)

ACME Financial will be provided with logo and naming identification as the title sponsor of the Centre on the soccer field concourse of the soccer fieldhouse. * (approximate size 2′ x 3′)

vi) Fieldhouse 2 – Gymnasium
ACME Financial will be identified with logo and naming identification as the title sponsor of the Centre on a wall banner on one of the main walls in the Gymnasium Centre Fieldhouse Gymnasium.

ACME Financial will be provided with logo and naming identification as the title sponsor of the Centre on the wall signage above the bleachers of the gymnasium fieldhouse. *(approximate size 16′ x 16′)

ACME Financial will be provided with logo and naming identification as the title sponsor of the Centre on the field scoreboards of the gymnasium fieldhouse. *

ACME Financial will be provided with logo and naming identification as the title sponsor of the Centre on the pull out bleacher signage of the gymnasium fieldhouse. *(size and number TBD).

vii) Running Track

ACME Financial will be identified with logo and naming identification as the title sponsor of the Centre on 4 wall banners in the running track area, one in each corner of the track in the Centre Fieldhouse 2 – third floor level.

viii) Other

The City will work with ACME Financial to create a mutually agreeable new building theme through the use of design graphics and signage for the building and the various defined recreational spaces within the complex.

ACME Financial will be identified with logo and naming identification as the title sponsor of the Centre on wall signage adjacent to the storefront school in the youth/education centre.

5. ON-SITE RIGHTS AND BENEFITS

Facility
The City will provide ACME Financial with the opportunity to **display** ACME Financial product and/or information on display racks at designated areas within the Centre. Costs of execution and marketing collateral are the responsibility of ACME Financial.

The City will provide ACME Financial with the opportunity to **survey** the audience on site up to two times per year at a designated area within the Centre. Costs of execution and surveys are the responsibility of ACME FINANCIAL.

The City will provide ACME Financial with the opportunity to **use one arena free** of charge for up to 3 hours per occasion 4 times per year subject to arena availability.

The City will provide ACME Financial with the opportunity to **use the gymnasium** for its employees or client function free of charge for up to 3 hours per occasion 4 times per year subject to gymnasium availability.

The City will provide ACME Financial with the opportunity to use either **fieldhouse** for its employees or client function free of charge for up to 3 hours per occasion 4 times per year subject to fieldhouse/gymnasium availability.

The City will provide ACME Financial with free of charge access to activity and or meeting rooms up to a maximum of 4 hours per use and 4 occasions per year, subject to availability. You are encouraged to use these occasions for staff development and training.

Other Rights and Benefits
ACME Financial will be identified as the title sponsor of the Centre with logo and naming identification on all employee clothing such as vests, jackets, golf shirts, hoodies, t-shirts, name badges, and hats in the Centre.

ACME Financial will be given a variable credit toward obtaining memberships to the Centre at no cost for their employees up to 3.5% of the annual cash value of the partnership excluding the value of this benefit.

ACME Financial employees will be given a special sponsor purchase rate of 20% off the retail value of memberships.

ACME Financial will be given 100 general facility admissions per year for its discretionary use.

The City will use reasonable best efforts to provide ACME Financial with cross-promotional rights to enable ACME Financial to participate in other sponsor facility promotions subject to other sponsors' agreement and subject to other exclusivities the City may have.

ACME Financial will be identified with logo and naming identification associated with 2 landscape trees outside the building in prominent locations at the main entrance.

ACME Financial will be identified with logo and naming identification associated with 4 litter receptacles outside the building.

ACME Financial will be identified with logo and naming identification associated with 2 landscape trees outside the building in prominent locations at the main entrance.

ACME Financial will be identified with logo and naming identification associated with 2 park benches outside the building in prominent locations near the build-ing.

ACME Financial will be identified with logo and naming identification associated with 2 picnic tables outside the building in prominent locations near the building.

ACME Financial will be provided with the opportunity for each of its local employ-ees to name a walkway brick outside the main entrance to the building.

ACME Financial will be identified with logo and naming identification associated with the main board room table in prominent meeting rooms within the complex.

The City will provide other rights and benefits to be mutually agreed upon based on ACME Financial business goals and objectives.

_____

* Indicates that sponsor required to provide camera-ready artwork for distribution to the City for this element in size and detailed specifications to be provided by the City in advance for distribution to the City for this element with size and detailed specifications to be provided by the City in advance if required.

* Should any right or benefit not be available due to circumstances beyond the control of the City, reasonable replacement value will be delivered by the City.

CONSIDERATION

THIS SPONSORSHIP OPPORTUNITY IS AVAILABLE FOR
A MINIMUM 25-YEAR TERM COMMITMENT

Total Program Value:
$285,000.00 per year (Based on industry standards evaluation)

INVESTMENT: $230,000.00 + HST per year

NEXT STEPS

We look forward to following up with you next week to review and confirm the proposal with you and discuss your continued interest in the partnership.

In the meantime, should you or a designate from your team have any questions or comments, please do not hesitate to contact us directly.

Yours truly,
John Smith
City Project Manager
Tel: 414-719-0555
jsmith3@pickurCity.ca
www.pickurCity.ca

FULFILLMENT SPREADSHEET

ABC CORP (DATED: MAY 12, 2009, COVERS 2010/2011)

TASK CATEGORY	ITEM DETAILS
WEB & EMAIL	Logo Recognition on each page of WSC site with link back to site & dedicated tab on page Inclusion of logo on email blasts in 2009 (3-6 mailings) and on all other promo material
SIGNAGE	8 coroplast signs to be placed in reg or keynote area Composite event signs will include ABC CORP logo as Host Venue Sponsor and Event Sponsor
BINDER & HAND OUTS	Can add brochure etc. to Reg. kit Can provide brochure etc. at each place setting for the 'closing session' Can place ad in binder ABC CORP logo on sponsor page of binder
CONTACT LIST	To receive hard copy of full contact list
RECOGNITION	As official host venue and event sponsor 2x verbal recognition 2 minute speech to full assembly
REGISTRATION RELATED	4 full registrants to Congress Response to registrants to include drive to ABC CORP website for accomodations
LOGOS	Have one jpg and one eps
PG NEWSLETTER	Advertorial in 2 editions
OTHER	Display booth for both days of Congress Enter to Win contest for ABC CORP 3 questions specific to ABC CORP in evaluation

TIME LINE	RESPONSIBILITY	STATUS	QUESTIONS OR COMMENTS
Mid March	Nicki		
April	Nicki		
15-Sep-09	DFIC rep	15-Sep	
15-Sep-09	Nicki		
15-Sep-09	DFIC rep	15-Sep	ie. Coupons
15-Sep-09	DFIC rep	15-Sep	
15-Sep-09	DFIC rep	15-Sep	
15-Sep-09	Nicki		
Sept 15 & Nov 1	Tricia		Should be soft copy?
At Congress	Brent or Steph		
At Congress	Brent or Steph		
At Congress	DFIC rep		
9/15/2009 ?	Nicki		Was 2 in 2009
	Tricia		
To us by March 1	DFIC rep		Confirm for 2010
	Nicki/Brent		
	DFIC rep		
At Congress	DFIC rep		

FULFILLMENT SPREADSHEET

XYZ CORP (DATED APR 14,09 APPLIES TO CONGRESS 2009/2010/2011) $5,000

TASK CATEGORY	ITEM DETAILS
WEB & EMAIL	Logo Recognition on each page of WSC site with link back to site Inclusion of logo in email blasts as workshop sponsor?
SIGNAGE	4 coroplast signs for reg. /main areas (supplied by XYC CORP) 2 coroplast signs for workshop (supplied by MD) Composite event signage to include XYZ CORP as workshop sponsor
BINDER & HAND OUTS	Can add brochure etc. to Reg. kit Can provide brochure etc. at each place setting for the workshop Can place ad in binder XYZ CORP logo on sponsor page of binder
CONTACT LIST	To receive soft copy of contact list Provide list of 5 Min Pitch panelists
RECOGNITION	Workshop Sponsor (category exclusivity) law firm review on 5 minute pitch, opportunity to review after sellers and buyer, note on website Verbal recognition at Congress 2 Minutes at workshops to promote XYZ CORP
REGISTRATION RELATED	6 registrations
LOGOS	Have jpg and eps
OTHER	Presenting speaker of workshop 10x20 booth at Congress

TIME LINE	RESPONSIBILITY	STATUS	QUESTIONS OR COMMENTS
March	Nicki		
	Nicki		
15-Sep-09	Jolan		
15-Sep-09	Jolan		
	Nicki		
15-Sep-09	Jolan		
15-Sep-09	Jolan		
15-Sep-09	Jolan		
	Nicki		
Sept 15 & Nov 1	Tricia		
by end of June	Nicki		
Done	Nicki		5 minutes to note legal red flags after pitching and buying
at Congress	Brent/Steph		
at Congress	Jolan/Nicki		
	Nicki/Jolan		
	Nicki/Jolan		Confirm for 2010
	Nicki/Jolan		
	Nicki/Jolan		

INDEX

2005 Canada Summer Games 32, 60
2010 Vancouver Olympics xi, 98
2012 London Olympics 93
Activation 11, 29, 31, 57, 58, 79, 83-103,
107, 110, 118, 125-127, 130, 131, 135,
137, 142
Air Canada Centre 101
Airdrie Festival of Lights 75
Ambush marketing 137
American Idol 126
Arts marketing 137
Assets 3, 4, 5, 6, 10, 12, 13, 15, 18, 19,
27,53, 55, 57, 60, 63, 64, 67, 68, 70, 75,
78, 80, 100, 107, 129, 135, 137, 138, 139,
141, 148

Banana Republic 30, 96
BATNA 137
Beiler, Cynthia 33
Being Erica 99
Bell Canada 90
Benefits xv, 8, 9, 10, 14, 44, 47, 53, 55-
57, 60, 64, 67-71, 73, 77, 79, 81, 87, 90,
93, 96, 100, 103, 107, 115-118, 123, 137,
138-142, 149, 159, 160, 169, 171
BHP Billiton 91
Bilodeau, Alexandre 98
Blue Planet 46
BMO 56

*BMO Financial Group North America
(BMO Harris Bank)* 56
BP Ride for MS 62
Brand xiii, 4-6, 9, 10, 13, 18, 23, 25, 29,
30, 31, 42-45, 46, 56, 58, 60, 62, 63, 67,
68, 75, 77, 79, 87, 89, 90, 91, 92, 93, 95,
96, 98, 100, 102, 103, 126, 127, 135, 137,
139, 141, 142, 160
British Petroleum 91, 93
Budweiser 30
Bundling 70, 100, 138

Calgary Flames 90, 103
Calgary Stampeders 125
Canadian Soccer Association 29
Canadian Sponsorship Forum ix
*Canadian Sponsorship Landscape
Study 2012* xiii
Canadian Tire 7, 46, 69
Canadian Western Agribition 30
Canadian Western Bank 41, 42, 96
Cause marketing 138
CBC 99
Chan Centre for the Performing Arts 5
CIBC 5, 30
CIBC Run for the Cure 5
City of Toronto 7, 46
Coca-Cola 30, 60, 75, 98
Co-sponsors 138

Cross-promotion 138, 170
CSR 138

Deepwater Horizon 91, 93
Didow, Lisa Marie 31
Discovery 6, 23, 29, 31, 32, 34, 35-49, 53,
55-57, 58, 59, 61, 62, 69, 70, 79, 80, 87,
89, 100, 107, 110, 135, 138, 159
Doan, Catriona LeMay 96
Dow Chemical 75

Edmonton Fringe Festival 94
Edmonton Marriott at River Cree Resort
132, 133
EnCana 39
Ennis, Toni 23, 46, 67
Event marketing 139

Farm Credit Canada 41, 43, 98, 103
Fas Gas 101
Fedak, Justine 56
Fire Within 39
Four Seasons Centre for the
Performing Arts 5
Fulfillment 18, 57, 105-120, 132, 139,
174, 176
Funtastic 132

Gainer the Gopher 125
geoLOGIC Systems 94
Guerilla marketing 139

Harvey the Hound 90
Harvey's 90
Homeless for a Night 96
Hospitality 11, 14, 15, 68, 89, 90, 95, 97,
99, 125, 139, 148, 149

IEG ix
In-kind sponsorship 139
Intangible benefits 139
Inventory 1-19, 40, 73, 137, 138, 139,
140, 146, 148, 150, 152, 154, 157

Keating, Sue 56, 107
KidSport Saskatchewan 97

Licensed merchandise 140
Listerine 94
Livegreen Toronto 7, 46, 69

MacEwan University 31, 132
MARCOM 31, 132
Mark's 29
McDonald's 98
McEwan, Jim 132
Media sponsor 16, 140
Molson Old Style Pilsner 95
Mott, Suzanne 4, 85
Moxie's 103

NASCAR 126

Parekh, Neil 3, 43
Partnership Group –
Sponsorship Specialists™ ix, 10, 13, 26,
32, 37, 40, 47, 48, 53, 58, 64, 67, 74, 81,
89, 90, 91, 94, 117, 133, 148, 157, 183
Pepsi 60, 70
Person, Daniel 42
Philanthropy xiii, 81, 87, 138, 140,
142
Podbielski, Ron 41, 43, 98, 103,
Potash Corporation 91
Presenting sponsor 5, 9, 16, 88, 96, 141,
150

INDEX

Primary sponsor 141
Property xiii, 3, 4, 6-29, 32, 33, 34, 43, 46, 47, 48, 53, 56-59, 62, 63, 64, 67, 68, 70, 71, 74, 80, 85, 87-91, 92, 93, 95, 97, 99, 100-103, 107, 110, 111, 120, 123, 125, 126, 130, 135, 137, 138, 139, 140, 141, 142, 147, 148, 150
Proposal 26, 33, 40, 42, 45, 47-49, 51-81, 87, 89, 107, 110, 129, 135, 138, 139, 141, 142, 143, 157-172
Prospect xi, 5, 6, 15, 21-34 (prospecting), 39-42, 45, 46, 47-49, 53, 56-59, 61, 63, 64, 67, 68, 70, 71, 73, 74, 75, 79, 80, 81, 87, 92, 94, 127, 135, 138, 139, 140, 141, 159

Ramada 30
RBC 6, 30
Remax 98
Rights fee 11, 58, 68, 88-92, 98-103, 137, 138, 141, 142
River City Casino 132
ROI xiii, 10, 74, 75, 81, 87, 91, 97, 100, 117, 120, 138, 141
Rotary ix
Rotary Four-Way Test ix

Saddledome 5, 90, 103
Saskatchewan Arts Board 30
Saskatchewan Blue Cross 96
Saskatchewan Credit Unions 30
Saskatchewan Roughriders 95, 97, 125
SaskEnergy 41, 43, 97, 98, 103
SaskTel 30, 39, 41, 43, 98, 103
Saveraux, Angela 41, 42
ScotiaBank Saddledome 5
Signage 7, 8, 11, 17, 43, 60, 67, 68, 75, 79, 87, 90, 97, 99, 110, 118, 119, 130,

140, 141, 143, 152, 154, 163-168, 174, 176
Simon Malls 126
SMCC Marketing Awards ix
SMCC One Day Sponsorship Training Workshops™ xiii
SMCC Western Sponsorship Congress xiii
Sponsee 142
Sponsorship Marketing Council of Canada (SMCC) ix
Sponsorship Toronto ix
Supplier ix, 6, 27, 31, 32, 40, 55, 57, 141, 142
Susan G. Komen for the Cure 62

TD Canada Trust 30
Tim Hortons 5, 100, 101
Timbits Soccer 100
Title sponsor 6, 29, 87, 96, 141, 142, 163, 164-169
Toronto Maple Leafs 101
Toronto Symphony 30, 96
Toshiba Canada 32

U.S. Cellular 33

Value xiii, 3, 4, 5, 6, 9, 10, 11-19, 43, 45, 59, 60-63, 67, 68, 69, 71, 73-77, 80, 81, 93, 95, 96, 97, 99-101, 117, 123, 126, 129, 130, 131, 132, 138, 140, 142, 143, 146, 148, 149, 151, 153, 155, 169, 170, 171, 172
Venue marketing 143
Vertigo Theatre 4, 85
Virtual signage 143

West Edmonton Mall 42, 65, 66

Westerner Days 101
Westerner Park 101
Winners 29
World Vision 3, 43, 64-66

Youth Empowerment &
Support Services (YESS) 96, 107

ABOUT THE AUTHORS

Brent Barootes is President and CEO of the Partnership Group – Sponsorship Specialists™, a Canadian national sponsorship consulting firm. In the past 25 years Brent has worked directly or indirectly with many Canadian brands, corporations, small and medium businesses as well as charities, nonprofits, professional and amateur sports teams, to develop, audit, enhance, design, and build effective sponsorship programs for them.

Janet Gadeski is President of Hilborn, an independent Canadian publisher serving the social profit sector. Her experiences in fundraising and nonprofit management range from a public radio station to performing arts and faith organizations. As founding president and CEO of The United Church of Canada Foundation, she helped to create a national foundation for the denomination and developed a low-cost, socially responsible investment program for its congregations.